MOANA

BOOKS ALSO BY DAWN BATES

Becoming Annie – The Biography of a Curious Woman (2020)

The Trilogy of Life Itself:

Friday Bridge – Becoming a Muslim, Becoming Everyone's Business (2nd Edition, 2017)

Walaahi – A firsthand account of living through the Egyptian Uprising and why I walked away from Islaam (2017)

Crossing The Line – A Journey of Purpose and Self-Belief (2017)

ALSO PUBLISHED BY DAWN PUBLISHING

Becoming the Champion – V1 Awareness by Korey Carpenter (2020)

Unlocked – Discover Your Hidden Keys by Carmelle Crinnion (2020)

Break Down to Wake Up – Journey Beyond the Now by Jocelyn Bellows (2020)

Slave Boy – Book 1 in the Democ'Chu Series by Nath Brye (2020)

MOANA

THE STORY OF ONE WOMAN'S JOURNEY BACK TO SELF

DAWN BATES

DAWN PUBLISHING

© 2020 Dawn Bates

Published by Dawn Publishing

www.dawnbates.com

The moral right of the author has been asserted.

For quantity sales or media enquiries, please contact the publisher at the website address above.

Cataloguing-in-Publication entry is available from the British Library.

ISBN: 978-1-913973-28-5 (paperback)
978-1-913973-01-8 (ebook)

Book cover design – Jerry Lampson
Publishing Consultant – Linda Diggle

Disclaimer: The material in this publication is of the nature of general comment only and does not represent professional advice. It is not intended to provide specific guidance for particular circumstances and should not be relied on as the basis for any decision to take action or not to take action on any matters which it covers.

CONTENTS

Dedicated to
Those afraid to break their silence
and
Those who have broken their silence

FOREWORD

According to surveys from six European countries, up to 20% of women in Europe have experienced trauma due to some form of sexual assault during their life[1].

According to OWH, Office on Women's Health, nearly 11 million women in the United States have been a victim of a DFSA, Drug-Facilitated Sexual Assault, meaning that the victims had been drugged in some way or were incapable of giving consent because they were under the influence[2].

According to a Canadian survey, one in three (32%) women have experienced unwanted sexual behaviour in public[3].

Those statistics are an underestimation, I believe the numbers would be much higher if everyone would report unwelcome sexual comments, actions, advances, and assaults. In my own experience in working with thousands of women, most of them have experienced trauma due to some type of unwanted sexual behaviour throughout their life, often going all the way back to when they were children.

Another statistic shows about 70% of adults in the U.S. have experienced some type of traumatic event at least once in their lives. This includes birth trauma, serious injuries, sexual, emotional, or physical abuse, medical procedures and the loss or death of a loved one.

Dawn shows us what is possible in this masterfully written and captivating volume. Through the lens of Moana we get to witness her riveting journey of self-healing, shadow work and trauma recovery from sexual assault.

As a time-line trauma release facilitator and teacher trainer I help people from all over the world to release their birth, childhood, ancestral and sexual trauma from their body, brain, and energy field. I see miracles happen every day when people are willing to do the work to heal their past, rewrite their story, step out of victim consciousness, and take back their power.

What is the definition of trauma? Imagine anything that is too intense or overwhelming to process or integrate in the moment that it is happening or shortly thereafter. It's important to understand that the physical body and especially the nervous system get profoundly impacted when we feel physically and/or sexually un-safe. When we feel threatened our body instinctually goes into a high state of arousal. The natural survival instinct kicks in, also known as the fight-flight-freeze or appease response. Imagine sudden tension in the muscles, hyper-alertness in the brain, the whole body is being mobilised to fight and/or escape, to play dead or become overaccommodating. The chemistry and physiology in the brain and body changes and every cell in your body is armouring up to protect itself. In an ideal situation, your body would guide you to discharge this build-up of energy and return to a natural equilibrium.

Unfortunately, most humans have lost the ability to trust the innate wisdom of the body and tend to hold on to the shields of protection long after the threat has come and gone. Some people live in constant survival mode, because the place they spend most of their time is not a safe space, like home, work, or school. This may lead to severe imbalances in the brain chemicals that modulate mood and behaviour and the ability to self-regulate, which is an essential key to being resilient.

In some cases we are also holding on to trauma that is not ours, it was passed on from generation to generation and projected upon us without our consent. The long-term impact of unhealed trauma leads to living life fully armoured, always ready to run, fight or appease in order to survive. The nervous system is under pressure and can potentially become oversensitive or desensitised and over time the trapped energy in the body and brain becomes toxic, creating disharmony and disease.

What are the benefits of de-armouring the body? This is core level shadow work, I once heard someone say, "The issue is in the tissue" and it's true! By shining the light of awareness on the pain and discomfort that is frozen deep inside the cellular memory, you can literally melt the frozen energy and restore and repair every cell in your body.

Body armour can impact any part of the body and is usually found in the fascia (connective tissue), the sexual reproductive system, the renal and endocrine system, the psoas muscle, the digestive system, and the vocal region. It is actually very interesting to look at a photo of the vocal cords, when you do a quick online search you will see it looks exactly like a yoni (vagina). I'm not surprised because there is a direct link between traumatic experiences and having the courage to speak up.

Communication is often the first step towards self-love, discernment, consent and creating and upholding healthy boundaries. Humans are also 'wired' for connection and the nervous system and the vagus nerve are key players. In case of unhealed trauma the nervous system can be oversensitive or numbed down. I encourage you to start from the inside out and first cultivate a loving relationship with yourself and your body.

On top of any trauma, women are bombarded with unrealistic body images, and trying to fit in can lead to body shaming and even self-loathing. Restoring the loving relationship with your own body is the gateway into learning about your body's consciousness and discovering its innate wisdom and capacity for self-healing. When you de-armour and reawaken your natural capacity to self-soothe and self-regulate the nervous system, in combination with reclaiming your voice, you are rebuilding resilience and increasing your chances to magnetise healthy and nourishing relationships into your reality.

I am excited for you to read this book as it offers tangible, meaningful insights that will help you to recognise the impact of unhealed trauma and show you the positive results of doing the shadow work.

You can use the book as a tool to illuminate unhealed

aspects in your body and energy field. Remember that your body is a powerful messenger and I encourage you to keep a journal as you read this gripping book. Set the intention to tune into your body, noticing any changes in muscle tension or restriction in your breath. This allows you to become more conscious of any body armour or shields of protection you are holding in your field.

One piece of advice, be gentle with yourself, ask your body to work with you without forcing anything.

The journey of trauma healing is like a magical soul retrieval, in which you welcome back all the parts of you that were left behind in time.

This book is more than a story, it is a teaching and it is my hope that Dawn's heartfelt sharing will grant all of you permission to be courageous enough to reset the template for yourself and for the future generations.

Love from my heart to yours,
Sandra Rolus
https://sandra rolus.com

---

1. www.emcdda.europa.eu/attachements.cfm/att_50544_EN_TDS_-sexual_assault.pdf
2. www.womenshealth.gov/a-z-topics/date-rape-drugs
3. www.150.statcan.gc.ca/n1/pub/85-002-x/2019001/ar-ticle/00017-eng.htm

ONE
THE NIGHT IN QUESTION

Leaving the meeting she was both excited and nervous.

The meeting had gone well, although some of the fellow school governors were so afraid of the system it was going to be hard to innovate and drive the school forward, but steps were being taken and things were moving in the right direction.

Working in the education system was so much slower than the world of entrepreneurship, and yet it didn't need to be. The dogma that came down through central government was limiting and stifling at best, so why did she want to be involved? Well that's just who she was, someone who wanted to improve on all aspects of society, create a powerful legacy so she could leave the world in a better state than when she had arrived.

Starting with the broken government schooling system so the kids whose parents couldn't afford private schools have similar opportunities, was a great place to start. She had made sure her two boys had been given as many opportunities as possible, and it broke her heart to see so many children go without. Reading the latest reports from the Local Education Authority had led to a heated debate at the last governor training meeting, and it had got her noticed, and shaken a few molecules of those who were not able to think about the greater impact, mainly in part due to the fact that it had been swallowed up by the system of academia.

Thinking about what was next on the agenda was a good way to distract her from the nerves she was feeling about this next meeting. She was meeting up with Joe, her ex, someone she had ended the relationship with just over a week ago after months of wondering why she was still with him. She had missed him, but equally she didn't want things to end as they had done. She had never been one for a bad ending… in a book, in a movie, and certainly not in her own life.

Walking out on him and leaving him in the pub, before going back to her home, packing his stuff up and leaving it outside her back door, then sending him a text message to tell him it was over had been a long time coming. He hadn't given her the support or the attention he had at the beginning, and their last trip up north had been the worst so far. Selfish, arrogant and intimidating were the three words she had narrowed it down to. He wasn't the man she had fallen in love with, and yet she had continued to stay with him because she thought she needed him, thought she had loved him; the truth was, she just wanted to be loved, wanted and desired. He had told her she was, in the beginning, but now he was more interested in drinking and hanging out with his friends.

Her phone pinged. It was a message from him. He had

arrived at the pub. She messaged back telling him she would be five minutes, and to order her a pinot gris. He messaged back saying it was already waiting for her. That made her smile. He had bought her a drink. Normally it was her that had to pay for everything. He hadn't contributed to very much at all over the time they had been together, always saying he didn't have the money. But the longer she had stayed with him, the longer she realised he always had money for beer. Most of his wages went on beer; another reason she had ended it.

Walking into the pub, she spotted him straight away. Her heart missed a beat. She knew the feelings she had for him were still there. Every time she closed her eyes, all she could see was his face, his smile, and his kind eyes. She had breathed in his scent so many times it was now her aroma of choice, reminding her of the novel *Perfume* by Patrick Suskind. She went in to kiss him, almost by default. And with a degree of hesitation he pulled away, told her, "Don't."

She dropped her gaze, felt a stabbing sensation in her heart, felt the tears prick the back of her eyes, but she understood. The last time they had seen each other was when she had sat across from him in another pub, the night she told him she'd had enough. He hadn't followed her, hadn't bothered to try and sort it out. He'd just carried on drinking, and when he returned home and found his stuff outside, he'd banged on the door so hard she thought he was going to smash it in.

Her boys had been woken up by the banging. The friend she was on a call with could hear him banging and shouting – and she wasn't even in the kitchen where the back door was, but in her room, with the door shut. His anger scared her. He was like a volcano about to erupt, keeping his anger silenced, simmering. She had already been on the receiving end of a drunken moment.

She sat down, apologised, and dropped her head, not wanting him to see the pain in her eyes. He knew he had control over her, and it felt like it was another one of his games she just couldn't escape from. The partner of his ex, the mother of his daughter, had already told her she had been brainwashed by him. Had he been right? Had she? She took a sip of the ice-cold pinot gris and sat back in her chair, closed her eyes and still she saw him smiling at her, with what she had believed to be love in his eyes. Wanted to believe. Had it ever been? Would she ever know?

She asked him how he was, he smiled and said he was okay. They exchanged small talk and decided on the restaurant around the corner for dinner. She had always wanted to go there for dinner. She had been there before for lunch and a coffee whilst writing and planning her future; a future that she had only seen with her and her dogs walking along the windswept cliff looking out to sea. No man. No one else around. That was until he had come into her life, and it seemed he was the perfect match, probably a little too perfect. Just like that saying goes he was probably 'too good to be true'.

As the night progressed, the laughter, lingering looks and conversation flowed, as if nothing had happened. It was a good night, and it was coming to an end. She had to get back to her children and her dogs, but there wasn't another bus for half an hour.

"Fancy one of those espresso martinis you love so

much, just to round off the evening?" Joe asked. "My treat."

Who was this man? Had he really changed in the last week and a half? He had just paid his share of the meal, wine before she'd even arrived, and now he was offering to buy her an espresso martini! "Okay, and then I have to get off as Abdu needs to get back to his."

After the final drink of the night, they stepped outside and started walking to the bus stop. He put his arm around her waist, pulled her in and kissed her. She melted in his arms. "It was really good to see you smiling and laughing again," he whispered into her ear, his hot breath sending shivers through her body.

Was it the drink? Or was it real? Her head spun in confusion, wondering what was happening. A rush of love? Confused, excited, afraid and not knowing what to do, and then they kissed. His lips so familiar, his arms so strong, his scent intoxicating her. Would she ever be able to break free from this love, the love of her life?

TWO

THE MORNING AFTER

Her hips hurt, her back ached, and her body was cold. What was that smell? She opened her eyes, tried to move, and then froze. Where the hell was she?

She turned her head to the right and saw his face. Fear paralysed her. The room started spinning and she felt sick. She had to get up, get to the bathroom, and then she noticed her skirt and underwear were missing. She tried sitting up, looking around for her clothes. She spotted her skirt. Where were her shoes? Where the fuck was she?

Trying to stand up, pain ripped through her body. She turned around and saw him coming to. She had no idea who he was; no idea where she was. She knew she would never have normally spoken with him or even wanted to come to a place like this. The next wave of nausea swept over her, her head pounding and spinning all at the same time. She went to grab her skirt and missed it. Her depth perception was off, way off. She went for it again, and nearly fell over. She grabbed onto the doorframe, the dirty, broken doorframe. A flicker of a thought came to mind of how it needed a good sanding down and varnishing.

Thinking of the smell of varnish was all it took for her insides to heave. She made it to the kitchen. Bare, dirty, and not a place she would want to eat a scrap of food. Where the hell was she? And why did she feel so spaced out? Why did her body hurt so much? She knew the answer but didn't want to know it.

Looking around this small grotty flat, holding onto what looked like a breakfast bar, she noticed the time. Her boys! She had to get home to her boys!

A young girl appeared in a doorway, "Morning."

"Who are you? And where am I?"

"I live here, you came home with my dad last night. Don't you remember?"

"NO. I need to get home. My boys. I need to get home. How do I get home? I don't even know where I am!" Tears fell from her eyes; fear gripped every cell in her body. What kind of mother was she? Had Abdu stayed when she hadn't returned? Were the boys alone? Had they walked the dogs? Her head started spinning again.

"Look, it's okay. I'll call my friend and he will take us back to get my car and then I will take you home," said the man as he came out of the room she had woken up in.

"Where are my shoes? Where is my bag? And my coat?" she cried out.

"You didn't have any of those with you. You must have left them in the club," he answered.

"What club?" A frown spread across her face, confusion setting in even deeper.

"The club on West Street."

"What club on West Street? What are you on about? I just need to get home. Please take me home."

"Do you remember where you live now? Because you didn't last night," he smirked.

"Of course, I know where I live! I just need to get home. I need to find my bag. Oh my God, what is happening here. How did I get here?" she cried, tears falling down her face.

"It's okay. You'll be okay," said the girl in the doorway, looking confused and concerned all at the same time.

With every movement she made, her whole body hurt, the room spun even more, and the nausea kept flowing over her like waves of the ocean.

"My friend is on his way. He'll be here in five minutes," said the guy she'd never seen before.

"Okay." But was it okay? Okay to get in a car with men she didn't know? Being driven home from only God knows where? She needed answers and she needed to get home.

"Where am I? Where are my things?" she asked noticing for the first time her speech was slurring, and her head was throbbing as well as spinning.

"You're in Stocksbridge, about eight miles from Sheffield," the girl replied. "Do you really have no idea where you are or what happened last night when you got home with my dad?"

"He's your dad? And no, I don't. The last thing I remember is heading home to my children. Oh my God, my children." With this, tears fell. Fear ripped through her body and she noticed the look of fear on the girl's face. "I need to get home. Where are my things?"

"You didn't have anything with you," said the guy, now

looking as scared as the girl. "Look, I can drop you off. My car is parked near the club you were in and we can ask them if they have your things. Just calm down."

"Calm down! I have no idea who you are, how I got here, why my body feels the way it does, where my things are and my children are either home alone or at school, and I feel like I am going to pass out at any minute – and you want me to calm down?" she screamed back at them.

"Kinda, yeah," said the guy looking out of the doorway before he turned around and said, "My mate is here, let's go."

The car which drove up did not belong in an area like this. Top of the range BMW with all the trims and alloys, all tastefully done and not at all bad boy. This was more than likely a drug dealer's car in this kind of area, and looking at the guy who drove it, he didn't belong here anymore, if he ever did.

"Do you need some water?" asked the driver.

"No thank you, I just want to get home and make sure my boys are okay, and my dogs. Is it okay if I have the window open? I feel really ill."

"You don't look well either love, so yeah, open the window," the driver replied. "So, you don't know how you got to my mate's house last night, or what happened?"

"No, I keep saying that. I have no memory other than walking to the bus stop with my ex to go home to my children." And with that, the tears started flowing again, even though she was trying to keep it together.

She noticed the look of concern on the driver's face, and the way he looked at the guy who's flat she had woken up in. "Are you okay love?" asked the driver, "You don't look too good."

"I just feel really out of it, I can't focus my vision and my body really hurts," she said between the tears. Every movement made her body hurt. Every bump in the road made her feel sick, and she felt like she had taken a nasty pill from back in the days of raving. That said, she had never felt this bad, not even after a bank holiday bender. This was out of it on a whole new level of awful.

"You said you were with your ex, where was he last night when you were at the club?" asked the driver.

"I don't even know which club you are on about, and I told you, the last thing I remember is walking to the bus stop to go home. And I don't know where he is, or why your friend here says I was on my own."

"You were on your own, and you were quite adamant that I took you home, but you had no idea where you lived, so you came home with me," said the guy from the flat.

"But I don't even know you – and, no offence – but you are not the kind of person I would normally speak to," she replied.

"You didn't belong in that kind of club either love, so I wouldn't worry about it. We'll just get you home and be done with it, yeah?" stated the guy from the flat, with what she detected was hesitation and nerves.

They had been driving for what seemed ages, through parts of the city outskirts she had only read about in regeneration reports, and not areas she would have wanted to walk alone in during the day – let alone at night.

She could see the city centre looming up ahead and started to recognise where she was. She knew they had taken the back roads, and in a car like this, there were only two reasons for that. One, they were keeping off the main roads for fear of being spotted – or two, the main roads were closed. The uneasy feeling in her was not subsiding, and why did this guy's daughter and his friend keep looking at him with fear and concern?

What had happened to her and why had she woken up in the condition and the state she was in? And, where was he? Where was Joe? Yet again, in his company and something bad happens to her. WTAF was it with him? Had she been cursed? Had he set her up? Had he spiked her? It wouldn't be the first time in his company she had been spiked. Why the hell did she stay with him? Why had she even asked to meet with him? Stupid! Stupid! Stupid! Like a moth to a flame, burnt by the fire… weren't they the lyrics to a song from back in her teenage years? Janet Jackson… or someone like that?

The car stopped on a side road off West Street. The guy showed her where they had met and suggested her things may still be inside. Looking at the club from the outside she knew it was not a place she would have ever gone to, not knowingly anyway. She had been in some dodgy places in her early twenties during her raving days, but this place? Not a place she would have ever chosen, for the look of the place or the music it played.

The guy was banging on the door to see if someone would answer, but no one did. He said he had to get back, and would drop her off at home. She looked at him, looked at the car door. Hesitated.

He looked at her, understanding her hesitation. "It's okay, just get in."

Head still spinning, confusion, excruciating pain beginning to rip through her body like she was in labour, she was stood on the side of the road getting into another car. A smaller one, and this time the guy from the flat was in the driver's seat.

"Tell me where you live, and I will take you home," he said as he turned the key.

She gave him directions between the waves of nausea and every bump in the road sending stabbing pains through her body. The next thing she remembered is seeing her apartment up ahead and the guy saying this was a completely different place to where she told him she lived the night before, when a taxi driver had driven them all over for about twenty minutes looking for her home.

She got out, thanked the guy for the lift and he sped off. She made her way to the back door, and couldn't get in. She didn't have a key, it was in her bag, but where was that? And her coat and shoes?

She made her way around to the front of the property and in through the front door of the apartments. Every step she took sent a sharp stabbing pain up through her body, her head throbbed harder, louder and caused the nausea to sweep over her in ways she had not even experienced with her migraines that had left her out of it for days on end. She got to the top of the stairs and reached for the spare key at the top of the door. Reaching that high had made the pain rip through her body so fiercely she felt the bile in her stomach reach the back of her mouth. She heard her dogs barking inside and she called out to her beloved fur babies, "It's okay, Mummy's home."

They were both excited to see her, and as she made her way into her apartment, she called out to her boys. They had left her a note: *Gone to school, see you when we get back. Love you xx.* Tears pricked her eyes and fell. She had such great boys, and they deserved so much better than her; I mean, what kind of mother allows something like this to happen to her?

Before she had even realised where she was, she was walking the dogs around the back of Tesco, a quick 20-minute walk, out of the view of prying eyes. She had no idea how she had got there, all she knew was as time went on the pain was getting worse, and she knew she'd had sex, and from the feelings she was experiencing, it wasn't pleasant either, or consensual; and in that moment she vomited.

Making her way back to her apartment with the dogs, her head was so spaced out. Her vision was so distorted, and she had no idea of depth perception. What on earth must she had looked like walking the dogs? Taking the leashes off her dogs, giving them a bone from the freezer, she went to lay down on her bed, but she felt so afraid of being on her own. She didn't want her boys to see her like this, and she didn't want to be on her own. Her room was spinning, walls falling in on themselves, this was a bloody bad trip if ever there was one. She knew she needed help, so making her way through the back door, and down the alley, she knocked on the door of the bakers next door.

As soon as the lady saw her, the shock on her face said it all. "Oh my God, what on earth has happened to you, my love? Come on, sit down. Here, have a cup of tea and a cigarette."

Fading in and out of consciousness, she managed to give the lady a telephone number to dial because she couldn't see the dial pad due to her distorted vision. Another cup of tea, more reassurance and now the bakery owner showing concern. This was not the neighbour they knew; this was not the lady they had become friendly with over the past few years. What on earth had happened to her? Bit by bit the three of them pieced together all the things she could remember. It was not a pretty story, and not the first one the two ladies had heard about the pub or the club she had been to; nor would they expect her to go to the club this guy had said she had gone to.

Several cups of tea later, and the phone of the bakery rang again. Her ex-husband was just getting off the bus. He was here to take care of her and get things sorted.

Emotions flooded her body. She felt safe knowing he was here, felt loved and knew she would be alright with him by her side. She always had.

Why had he ended their marriage?

Things had gone so badly since he told her he wanted a divorce, but she was the kind of woman who would make a positive out of everything, including this current situation. How long that would take though was anyone's guess.

THREE

THE EX-HUSBAND

"I... I... I need... will you help me please?" She had asked through tears. "I need help, and I didn't know who else to call. Please?" She had begged him.

"Where are you?" Abdu asked.

"I'm at home, well the bakery next door. The ladies here are taking care of me."

She cried all the way through the call. She could hear the concern in his voice and when he said he would be there in 30 minutes, she thanked God they had worked together on salvaging a great relationship after their 15-year-marriage had ended in divorce just four years earlier.

"Stay where you are. I'm leaving now."

The moment he saw her, he was taken aback. She knew she didn't look good at all. She didn't realise she still had leaves in her hair. She thought her and the ladies had gotten rid of those. Her face was all puffy from crying, her eyes filled with fear and the unknown, and she smelled like a stinking ashtray with the lingering smell of a pub. This was not her. She was always so clean and tidy.

What the fuck had happened to her?

"I… I… I couldn't remember anyone's number but yours, I'm so sorry. I didn't know who else to call, or who else to trust," she said breaking down in tears.

He put his arms out and she fell into his arms. Wrapping his arms around her, he held her tight, promising to keep her safe. He would make sure he did whatever she needed. What had happened to her? As he moved his hands up and down her back she flinched.

"What's happened to you? Can you tell me?" he asked her softly. His eyes full of kindness, and a hint of anger.

They knew each other so well, and as tears fell she said, "I don't know, but I hurt all over; especially down there."

Her body shook with tears and he held her tighter, taking care not to hurt her more than she was already hurting.

The rage grew inside of him, but he kept his calm. He had learnt to. Nothing like this had ever happened to her whilst they had been together, but since him, nothing but trouble; and it wasn't just her it affected, it was his children; their children. Someone had hurt her badly, that was obvious. And yet again the prick she had been seeing wasn't there to keep her safe.

He checked himself, this wasn't about him or Joe; it was about her and what she needed. "Go clean yourself up and have a hot shower; or did you want me to run you a bath? Actually, have a shower, and then if you want one, have a bath, will be more relaxing for you. I'll make you a cup of tea and then figure what to do next."

For the first time since he had known her, she didn't want a bath. It had been painful enough to get in the shower. As he was making the tea, she tried to explain to him what had happened. She was all over the place. She was so spaced out it actually scared him. What the fuck had she been given? He knew she wouldn't have taken anything, not these days. Back in the day, yes, but not now. She was on too much of a mission to even have an afternoon nap, let alone a day off sick or dealing with a comedown. Some bastard had spiked her! And she had been with that loser! WTF? Why hadn't he taken care of her? Protected her? What the fuck was she doing with him? She was way out of Joe's league… and now his lack of care and responsibility had caused some other arsehole to violate her and abuse her.

He watched her move and knew that she was bruised in all the areas she shouldn't be. He could see bruises appearing on her neck where someone had had their hands around her neck. He scanned the rest of her skin to see if he could see any other bruises. There were bruises around her biceps where she had been pinned down, and again on her forearms. His anger was rising even further; directed at Joe, the thugs that had hurt her… and at himself. No harm had ever come to her when they were together, and if they hadn't got divorced, she wouldn't be hurting now.

As she sat down, he could tell it was painful. What the fuck had they done to her? His heart was breaking. Her tears coming again with the realisation that something really nasty had happened to her. How was she going to heal from this? How could he help her deal with this? What role could he play in her life now and in the future?

As she explained what had happened, he offered to go

to the place where the guy from the flat said they were last night. He called the club and the woman who answered confirmed her laptop bag and phone were still there, with her coat. He told the woman he would be there in 25 minutes. When he told her the stuff was there, she shook her head in confusion.

"It's not even a place I knew existed, or a place I would go to. Why would I be there? How did I get there?" she questioned through tears.

He sat beside her and placed his arm around her, pulling her closer. He kissed the topped of her head. "Everything will be okay. I'm here for you. I promise. No one can hurt you again."

She hugged him back; feeling safer than she had felt in such a long time.

As she finished her tea, he told her to lay down on the couch and he put a blanket over her. "Lock the doors from the inside, and I'll knock and call out when I get back. Do not let anyone else in, okay? I'll be back in about 40 minutes. In fact, where are the spare keys? I reckon you should lie down after your shower. Will you be okay? Is it okay for me to come back in if you are sleeping? I don't want to scare you."

"Yes, I'll be okay. Thank you, Abdu. For coming over, for helping me."

"Don't mention it. Just lie down. I'll be back within the hour." He gave her another hug and kissed her forehead, and then left her apartment.

As he descended the stairs, he realised he was crying. He had never seen her in such a state. His heart was breaking, and he knew he didn't want to see the jerk she had been seeing. He would lay into him; wanted to kill him. The crap she had dealt with since he came into her life. The moment he found out they were seeing each other he knew it wasn't a good thing. He didn't think it would last, thinking it was just a rebound thing, but they had been together over a year. He was irresponsible, childish, and incredibly selfish. She was more responsible than anyone he had ever known, was a great mother, and yet here she was selling herself short on this arsehole.

Thoughts of what he would do if he saw the arsehole she was with now consumed his mind. He didn't want to see him. He didn't want to know where he was. He would hurt him, and badly. But where was he? Why had he left her alone? Why had he not kept her safe? Had he been the one to hurt her? At this thought the rage bubbled over and he started shaking. He felt the heat rise in his face, his jaw tightened and his hands formed into a fist. "Breathe, you fool. He's not worth going to prison for," he told himself. All that matters is that she recovers and feels safe; feels supported.

And he promised himself he would not let her down again.

Hearing the knock at the door, she froze. Her hands started shaking and chills ran down her spine. "Get a grip on yourself," she told herself. "You are safe. No-one can hurt you. You're at home."

Was being at home going to keep her safe? She had always felt safe in the local area, and that hadn't kept her safe. She knew she would never have another alcoholic drink as long as she lived. She would never leave her drinks alone in a public place, even with friends. She didn't even want to go to a cafe bar again, was apprehensive about even walking the dogs. Still the dogs would let her know if the person outside was a familiar face, otherwise they would be barking like crazy.

Being at home drifting in and out of consciousness, the room spinning and every movement piercing her body, desperately trying to remember what had happened, she felt numb. Her fur babies snuggled up to her, one in her arms the other by her feet, she knew she was safe.

How had a really great day turned into this? Less than 24 hours ago, she had been prepping her boys' dinner, ready to head out for a school governors meeting. Twelve hours ago, she had been laughing with him. What had happened? Why could she not remember? Nausea swept over her body once more. She tried to get up, but the longer she was awake the more pain she was in. What had happened to her down there?

Him. He. The ex. She still found it hard to say his name. Joe, a name ruined forever, tainting her first impressions of others by the same name, if only for a split second whilst the memories of him subsided.

"Moana? Are you there?" called a male voice she recognised with another knock at the door. The dogs barking – but not aggressively, both excited – she snapped out of her thoughts and slowly made her way to the door. She let him in.

"Moana? Are you okay? You've gone really pale." At that moment, her legs buckled, and Abdu reached out and caught her. His arms wrapped around her and holding her tightly, he led her into the lounge and sat her down on the couch. "Let me get you some water."

She was in a daze, totally confused. She felt numb and as though she was outside of her body looking in on her life. How did he find her? Why was he here? She started shaking and before she knew it, she was crying, sobbing uncontrollably.

Abdu rushed back into the room, glass of water in hand. He sat next to her, put his arm around her and pulled her close to him, her head on his chest. "How did you find me? How did you get here?"

"It's alright, you're in shock. I went to get your things remember. Here, drink your water, and then check everything is in your bag."

Whatever she was dealing with, he wouldn't let her go through it alone. She needed someone to help her, and that is just what he was going to do.

"Is there anything else I can do? What about dinner? Did you want me to take the boys for dinner? Let you get some rest?" Abdu asked.

Then it hit her. The boys, what would they think of her when they got back from school? Tears started falling again.

"Hey, it's alright. Don't worry about the boys, they will be fine. We'll just tell them you have one of your migraines again. And I know you probably haven't thought about it, but did you want me to call the police for you? What about going to the hospital because you need to get checked out, for many reasons."

She knew he was right; she did need to get checked over, but how and where? There was no point going to the police because she didn't remember anything. What could she say to them? "Oh, by the way officer, I went out for dinner with my ex and woke up in a dirty skanky flat somewhere I don't know and left my two children alone all night?" They would love that, and the next thing she knew her children would be taken off her and she'd be up for neglect. "I don't want to involve the police; I don't remember anything anyway. So, what can they do?" she said as pain tore through her body even without her moving.

"Okay, but you need to see a doctor," Abdu said as he was searching Google for ideas. "Look the boys will be home soon, why don't I make some dinner for us all? Then I'll have to leave as I have got a meeting later."

"Okay. I think I want to be in bed when the boys come home, I don't want them to see me walking like this."

With that, Abdu helped her up, through the apartment and into bed. Then he started making dinner for the boys and him, as Moana didn't want anything and was already drifting off to sleep.

She felt the kiss of her boys on her forehead, and telling her not to worry, they would be fine, they would walk the dogs and just to let them know if she wanted a cup of tea. She thought she could open her eyes, but she didn't need to, she could already see through her eyelids, she could already see their faces; in fact, she was floating up above herself watching it all happen beneath her. What the fuck was going on?

"Baaba has cooked for us, and he's gone to his meeting now. He said he would call and check in on you later. Are you okay? Did you want a cup of tea?" asked her eldest. Waiting for a reply she couldn't give him, he kissed her on the forehead again and told her to get better soon. "I'm going to walk the dogs in a bit so if you hear the door, don't worry, it will just be me."

Murmuring something back to him, he told her to rest and get some sleep. He would make sure they got up for school the next morning and would make their lunch and put it in the fridge before he went to bed.

Feeling so proud of her boys, but unable to focus on her eldest as he reassured her, her heart exploded in love and pride for them both. Thank God they didn't know why she was really laying here in bed completely out of it.

Her ex-husband had taken such great care of her, made sure they kept this secret from their boys, and sorted out getting her stuff back. For the first time in a long time, she felt loved, genuinely loved. This deep friendship they had created made her feel safe. Everything just felt natural, and she was glad he had come to her when she needed him.

FOUR
THE NEXT DAY

She lay there, gripped with fear and shame. What had happened? How had she got here? Tears rolled down her face as she pulled her bedsheet up to her face and the fear took over. Anything could have happened to her. She had no memory, and no one to help her recover them. Did she even want to remember? What if the memories were removed for a very good reason? Maybe it was a blessing that she had no recollection of the evening?

She cried from the very depth of her soul. From the very core of her being and yet no sound came out. It was hard for her to even breathe. She felt as though she had a hand around her throat, tightening with every moment that passed. As she cried, she pulled her legs up and curled her body into the foetal position. Thoughts racing through her mind, fear consuming her, she felt dirty, shameful, and unworthy of being loved.

What was she going to do? How could she get help when she had no idea what had happened? She had no idea where to even go. How would she start to recover from this, if she could ever recover? The damage had been done, not just in a physical sense, but emotionally, mentally, and socially. She would never be able to trust herself again. How could she? She'd trusted in herself and now look at what had happened. She felt herself shrinking, her beautiful light going out and the darkness filling her up from the inside. She was lost forever, in the darkness of her own shame.

Her fur babies were laying on her bed, one by her side and the other by her feet, and at the first sign of her moving, they both made their way up to her chest and lay their heads on her, looking at her with sad eyes.

Beside her she saw a note on the pillow next to her. It was from her boys telling her that they had taken the dogs for a walk, gone to school and left the dogs with food in their bowls. They had also charged her phone and made her a bottle of water, which was on the ottoman toy chest beside her bed. They were such mature boys, more responsible than most men in their early twenties. She was so proud of them both.

As she tried to reach over to the phone, a pain shot up through her body, making her cry out. She didn't know if it was better when she was out of it, at least then she didn't feel the pain as much.

She needed the loo, but due to the pain it took her ages to get there, and when she was there, the pain she felt as she sat down on the toilet reminded her of childbirth. The stinging she felt as she peed was like nothing she had ever experienced and wiping herself with her non-perfumed wet wipes hurt like hell.

She made her way slowly back to her bedroom,

stopping off to make some fresh coffee. Even standing was too much for her. She wasn't comfortable lying down, standing up, sitting down, or walking. Taking her phone out of her pyjama pocket, she looked to see if she had a message from him. She hadn't heard from him the day before, but now she noticed a message from him.

I can't send you a message on Facebook.

Have you blocked me?

Do you have a problem with me?

She had no memory of blocking him. No memory of seeing this message, even though it looked like she had responded to him and unblocked him.

Apparently, he had woken up in a shop doorway with blood all over him, not his. Their friend had found him, the same friend who had picked him up the night she had ended it. He too was spaced out and had no idea of what had happened to him.

What the hell was going on in her head, and her heart? She had told him she was at home and not well. He had replied he was coming over.

Her whole body was telling her to stay away from him. To not speak with him in person or by message, so she closed her Facebook app and went into her room with her coffee.

Was it just an act? Could they have both taken something? If so, who had they gotten stuff from? She didn't know of anyone in Sheffield to get stuff from, had never known anyone in Sheffield. The last time she had done anything which would have even a remotely similar effect to this was back in her raving days, before the children were born; or when in a club, and she hadn't been out clubbing for well over a year, and that was only to help a friend out on the door of the club.

She did her best to get dressed, it took ages. Every movement sent pain through her cervix, her hips hurt like hell, and her arms and neck ached. As she dressed she noticed the bruising on her arms and legs, on her body. Tears and the howling coming out of her surprised both her and the dogs. What had happened to her? Then she noticed the bruising on her ankles. Tears and a silent scream came from the depths of her soul. Looking around her room in desperation for someone to hold her, to comfort her, and no one, only her dogs, she pulled them closer to her, their tongues washing away her tears telling her it would be alright. Would it be alright? Would she be alright? She needed to call someone. She needed to get seen by a doctor, she needed help.

There had to be someone who would be able to help her. An organisation, a helpline. Anything.

Searching through the rape crisis centre numbers, she avoided the local ones. She had worked with a few on some of the community projects she had mentored on and fundraised for. She didn't want to see someone she knew. Then she saw a number. Should she call it? What would they say? What would they think? What would they do? Her logical mind kicked in, if only long enough to make the call. Choosing a national number, she pressed the corresponding numbers on her phone. She had several attempts as she couldn't see the numbers due to the tears.

"Hello?" said a soft and kind voice on the other end of the phone. "How can I help you?"

She couldn't say anything. Tears just fell from her eyes,

and even crying hurt her body. "I… I… I need to see someone."

"It's okay my lovely. Are you safe right now? Are you with someone who can help you?" asked the lady on the phone.

"No, my chil… my children are … are at school. I am alone," she replied.

"Okay my lovely, don't you worry. What happened? Can you tell me?" enquired the soft voice.

"I don't remember anything. I just know I feel really out of it, and… and I am in a lot of pain… down below." Just speaking it out loud made her cry even more.

"Okay, my lovely. This is what we are going to do. You are going to tell me where you live, and I will send you a taxi and you will go to one of our centres who will help you, okay?"

"Okay. But what about my boys? What about my dogs?" Moana asked.

"Is there someone who can look after them when they get home from school, my lovely?"

"No, well yes, maybe. Their dad. I can call him and ask him."

"Well you do that then, and then I will call the taxi and then I will call you back. Okay? Is that okay my lovely? Don't worry, we'll get you sorted, don't you worry," reassured the kind aunty-type lady on the other end of the phone.

Moana messaged Abdu to let him know what was happening. He said he would head to her apartment after his meetings, take the dogs for a walk and meet the boys from school. He asked if she wanted him to make dinner for her as well as him and the boys. She wasn't sure what she wanted so told him to just sort himself and the boys out.

The dogs were busy knawing on a bone, looking up at her to make sure she was okay. Wagging their tails to let her know they were more than happy, and that the marrowbone was good. She smiled, for the first time since waking up the morning before, she had smiled.

The phone rang. It was the lady again. The taxi would be arriving any minute and would take her to an address where she would meet another lady who would take care of her and the situation. The lady wanted to stay on the phone whilst Moana made her way to the taxi. Moana waved to her dogs, as bending over to cuddle them as she would normally have done wasn't an option; not that the dogs minded they were too busy with their bones.

She locked her apartment door and slowly made her way down the stairs to the entrance door of the apartment block. The lady on the phone heard her pain and was reassuring her all the way down the stairs. Arriving at the taxi, the lady made sure the taxi driver had the correct address, just a number. No name. Just a number and an address, and the lady said, "Yes, that's it. Remember, you are going to be okay my lovely. I will call you back tomorrow to make sure you are okay, and I will call the centre now for them to let me know when you arrive. I know it doesn't seem like it now, but everything is going to be just fine."

FIVE

THE FORENSICS

Arriving at the centre her stomach was in knots.

What was going to happen?

How long would this take?

How many people would be there?

She had been promised there would only be women there and that she would be safe, the lady had been very kind on the phone.

As soon as she pressed the intercom button a friendly voice answered, "Hello?"

What was she supposed to say? Did she reveal her name? "It's me, it's…"

"It's okay lovely, no need to say the rest of your name. I'm on my way down."

Within moments a friendly face appeared to open the door.

As soon as she was inside, the lady put her arm around her and offered her a cup of tea and a biscuit. She was shown to a room, clean, airy and comfortable. Before the lady, who had introduced herself as Hema, went to make the cup of tea, two other ladies came in and introduced themselves.

One was a forensic doctor named Nikky and the other was a gynaecologist named Emmy. All three of them looked at her with sad kindness in their eyes, not pity, or disgust, or judgement, just sad kindness. She burst into tears and Hema immediately put her arms around her and told her everything would be okay. They would take things one step at a time, and EVERYTHING she said would remain confidential. They would also stop at any time when SHE wanted them to.

Having composed herself, Hema getting the tea, she sat opposite Nikky and Emmy. Nikky started taking all her details, reassuring her that she didn't have to give any details she didn't want to give, but the more information they had the better they could support her.

She didn't give her full name, or her full address. She only gave her real date of birth and occupation. Revealing this made her break down in tears even more. None of this could come out publicly. She had children and did not want this coming to light. She knew how the media worked. She also didn't want to be seen as tainted goods.

Which reminded her, where was he?

Why had he not been over to see her, especially when Abdu had come over straight away?

That had spoken volumes to her. Abdu was there like a shot, Joe nowhere to be seen. He obviously didn't care about her as much as he pretended to.

Oh, why had this happened? Why had she fallen for someone who enjoyed getting so drunk he'd left her alone, and not just on this occasion, on many? And this wasn't the first time this had happened. It had happened on their first holiday together too.

She had known then she needed to end it. But she didn't.

She knew when he tried to strangle her on their second holiday – drunk and high on whatever it was he had taken – that she needed to end it. But she didn't.

Why did she think so little of herself that she would stay with a man who wasn't there to take care of her?

She wanted someone who would protect her, make sure she was safe. He didn't love her the way she needed – or wanted – loving, and with these thoughts the wave of tears and emotions overcame her again.

Nikky and Emmy told her to take her time. Hema held her hand and told her she was safe; and with this small act of kindness, all of what had just gone through her head came out.

Where had he gone? They had been having such a lovely evening, and had been heading home. How had she got to this other place? And why had the guy told her she had been alone? Nothing made sense to her. Her whole body ached, hurt in places it shouldn't do and the room was distorting in places and moving around. This wasn't normal. What had happened?

After a couple of hours, several cups of tea, lots of tears, she had finally finished telling them what she remembered – and what the guy had told her had happened.

"So, let me see if I have got this right so far," said Emmy softly. "You went out to meet your partner, had a glass of wine before walking around to the restaurant to have a meal together. You enjoyed a couple of hours there, sharing a bottle of wine between you both, and then went back to the pub you started at whilst waiting for the bus home. You left and remember walking to the bus stop to go home as you needed to walk your dogs and be there in the morning for your boys; because your ex-husband had to get back to his place. Am I correct so far?" Emmy smiled.

She nodded, so Emmy carried on, "You say you then woke up in this flat, next to a guy you did not know, without your underwear on, and without your skirt. He told you that you hadn't been wearing any shoes. You said the flat was dirty and only a one bedroom flat. You said this man had his 18-year-old daughter sleeping in the next room, and the room you were in was the front room, not a bedroom?"

She nodded, tears streaming down her face. How could she end up in a place like that, let alone with someone she didn't know, and with no shoes?

Nikky reassured her, "Your memory loss is something that concerns me, and the fact that you are so spaced out. Without taking a blood test, which we will do shortly, it seems to me that you may have been spiked one of the many date rape drugs – but like I said, we won't know until we've done the blood tests. Please do not blame yourself. We are seeing an increase in this, and there is no shame in what has happened to you. Did you want to take a break? Can we get you a cup of tea?"

She shook her head, "No I want to carry on. I want to get this over and done with."

Emmy continued, "You said the man you were with told you that you had been in a local club, alone, and that you had been thrown out of the club, but he didn't say what for. He then told you that you demanded to get into the taxi with him to take you home. He then told you that you had no idea where you lived and they drove around the area you said you lived in for about 20 minutes."

Nikky and Emmy both looked at each other and then at Hema. There was confusion and concern in their faces.

"He then said he would take you back to his, not the police station, and then you walked up the stairs to his flat, which was on the first floor. It was only when you woke up in the morning, yesterday, that you realised you were 12 miles from home, in an area you had never been before, and had no way of getting back. This man then called his friend, who had a top of the range car, and offered to take you back to the place where you and this man met to see if you could obtain your bag and your coat. The place was closed, so this man then walked you back to his car and drove you back to your home, which was in a different place to where you had told them you lived the night before. You managed to enter your home after locating your key from the family known hiding place. You then walked the dogs in a daze, then went next door to the bakery, and the woman saw instantly the kind of state you were in. She allowed you to use her phone. The only person's number you could remember was your your ex-husband's, and not the ex you had been out to dinner with. You called him and he came over straight away. You said you felt really spaced out and sick. When your ex-husband arrived, he held you to comfort you. He then supported you by making you tea, before finding the number of the club this guy had said you were at. He then contacted the club where you had met this guy, and someone answered. He explained to them you had lost your laptop bag, coat and shoes and asked them to check if these items were in lost property. They confirmed they were, so whilst he arranged to collect them, you had a shower and put your clothes in the wash. He also told you he had contacted your ex-partner via Facebook but had not had a response."

She had sat nodding and confirming the details as Emmy was repeating them.

It was all so wrong. How had she gotten herself into this situation? She was always so careful. She was a good girl, always had been. She was the one other people looked up to, and now this? She felt broken, disgusted with herself. She had let her boys down, her parents down and herself down. She was supposed to have been home looking after her boys and the dogs, and whilst they were sleeping peacefully in her apartment, she had been lying on the floor in some dirty flat with a guy she wouldn't have normally even spoken to, let alone gone to his flat! It was a dirty, low class flat that looked like it was used more often than not as a place to enjoy drugs and whores rather than live in with your daughter. Was that just the snobbery in her?

So many thoughts cascading through her mind, none of them stringing together. She was scared. She was ashamed of herself. She was dirty, and she felt worthless.

And he still wasn't by her side. Why on earth was she with him?

With all the details down on paper, the ladies told her they were going to take a short break. Time for her to have a cup of tea and take a moment, whilst they prepared the examination room.

Hema took her hand and gently held it. "It's going to be alright. You'll move past this and you will become stronger, trust me."

She looked into Hema's eyes and saw the inner wisdom, a wisdom of experience, a wisdom that made her connect with her soul. She saw a remembering, a deep ancestral guide awakening within herself. A calmness fell over her and Hema nodded.

"You know what you need to do sweetheart, the answers are within you, and your soul sisters and wise women are here to help guide you, to support you, to heal you. Return to them and allow yourself to be guided, to be healed."

She nodded, and both her and Hema embraced each other. A deep connection only their people truly understood. She nodded, and for the first time since she woke up in that god-awful place, a smile tried to break across her face. A small one, not one of her big beaming smiles, but a smile none the less.

"When you walk through that door to where Nikky and Emmy are, you know that at any time you want them to stop, you just say so. It will take a couple of hours, maybe three or four, depending on what they find as they go along. But you set the pace. You are in control of this whole process. You do know that, don't you?"

She nodded. She knew, she understood. She knew that for the next few hours she was going to be examined like never before, and she knew before they had even begun, she would never want to be examined in this way ever again.

As Nikky walked back into the comfort lounge, she looked up. It was time. Hema walked with her and then went to get changed into her scrubs; something Nikky and Emmy had already done. She was asked to undress fully and put on a gown. Nikky talked her through the process. First, they would take her height and weight, her blood pressure, measure her heart rate and then they would ask her to lie down on the bed whilst they combed through her hair and cleaned under her nails. They advised her that because she had showered there may not be much, if any physical evidence, but it was worth doing, just in case.

It hurt her to walk, the pain shot up through the centre of her body, and when she climbed upon the bed, the pain ripped her insides. What had he done to her? Why did it hurt so much? She cried out in pain, fear and shame. How could there be this much pain?

Hema was back in the examination room and by her side. "Breathe my darling, take in the air you need. Oxygen, it will help you heal, my love."

Hema took her hand as she lay on the bed, looking up to the ceiling as if it was the night sky and the stars were shining down on her. She could hear Hema's voice; she could hear Emmy and Nikky reassuring her, one combing her hair, the other cleaning under her nails.

"This is the worst manicure and hair treatment I have ever had," she said as tears still fell.

"That's it, find yourself, find a way of dealing with it, of healing from it. Find yourself, my love," soothed Hema.

Hema's kindness and the spirit within her soul was so

warming, so healing. Her courage grew, if only by a little, but with each breath, with each molecule of oxygen that entered her body, she promised herself she would grow stronger. She would use this to become a wise woman, a wiser woman. This had happened to her for a reason, or rather happened for her for a reason.

With her hair combed and nails cleaned, Nikky then asked her to open her mouth as they were going to swab the inside, and they also asked her to allow them to swab just inside of her nose. Emmy told her to just lie where she was and take a moment whilst they recorded, bagged up and sealed the results of the examinations that had been done. Once they had done that, they were going to ask her to stand up again so they could take photos of her bruises.

"I know it hurts you to move sweetheart, but after you have moved off the bed to stand up so we can take the photographs, there will be just one more bed to lie on whilst we finish, okay?"

She nodded, looking over to the 'bed' Emmy had looked at whilst doing her best to reassure her. It was a bed with stirrups, one they used for taking smear tests and inserting the contraceptive coil, and she guessed some women also gave birth in chairs like this. She had never seen one before, even though she'd had two children. The first birth was a water birth, the second an emergency c-section. Seeing this chair, she was glad she had gone with the water birth.

"It's okay love, I know it looks horrible, but you just take your time and remember, you are in control of this process," Hema said as she gently wiped the tears away from her face.

She hadn't realised she had started crying again. Had she even stopped? Was this even real? It reminded her of the crime shows she had seen on TV… what was it? *Law and Order: SVU*? So, she was a 'special victim' was she? Another statistic in the crime database. Another number and reference to be known by within the system.

Nikky came over with a camera in her hand and started to demonstrate how she needed her to stand. "This way we can show the bruises accurately against this measure on this ruler we have, because we are going to have to document the size and shapes of them." Her smile was so caring and yet pitiful all at the same time.

She didn't want pity, she just wanted… she didn't know what she wanted. She just wanted to curl up and go to sleep; wake up and have this all be a nightmare that had never happened. She felt so alone. Tears started falling, would they ever stop?

It was only as Emmy held the ruler to her body that she realised how many bruises she actually had, and how big they were. She tried not to visualise the bruises, but with the shapes and measures being confirmed between Nikky and Emmy it was hard not to. The tears fell harder. What had he done to her?

The lumps on her head were measured and photographed, recorded and examined more carefully. She was asked if they hurt and what kind of pain it was. She hadn't realised there were so many. She knew her head was pounding but thought that was because of the drugs that had been put into her drink without her knowledge. There was no way she would have taken anything; it wasn't who she was any more. She didn't even like taking paracetamol when she got a headache.

"We're going to have to ask you to lie down on the bed for us to take the remaining photos," Emmy said placing a comforting arm around her. "Are you okay to do that for us?"

She nodded. She just wanted to get done what was needed to be done and leave, although she didn't want to leave. She felt safe here.

As she lay down on the next bed, Nikky demonstrated again how she wanted her to position her body so they could photograph and measure the remaining bruises on her inner thighs and around her vaginal area. Bruises on her vaginal lips? A huge wave of fear and tears overcame her and her body shook with convulsions. She knew she had been violated, she felt it with every movement but to hear her sacred space was now bruised was just too much.

Nikky stopped, nodded to Emmy and to Hema and let her know they were going to take a break. Hema said she was going to go and get a cup of tea and a chocolate biscuit, whilst Emmy held her hand and Nikky reassured her that she was being incredibly strong, one of the bravest women they had come across. She didn't know whether to believe them or not, so she just nodded; and as if Nikky had read her mind, "You may think we say that to all the women and young girls that come through here, and we do tell them they are being strong, brave and courageous, but you are different. You have something within you that just engulfs us all. YOU ARE STRONG, incredibly so; and the bravery at which you have shown for us to have accomplished all these examinations in such a short space of time, it's inspiring, please believe me. I've done this work a long time and you are one of the strongest and bravest I've ever seen. You've been through a lot, I can tell that just by looking at your injuries, and not knowing what has happened to you, I can see you trying to make sense of it all. All I ask is you be kind to yourself. This WAS NOT YOUR FAULT. These date rape drugs are everywhere, and it takes a split second. You trusted your drink with your ex. It could have been anyone asking for a light for a cigarette, or asking to use a chair from your table. It would have taken them a split second to put something in your drink whilst one of them distracted him. Do NOT blame yourself. Please?"

She nodded. She knew what Nikky was saying was true, she had been fully aware of the way things happened just from some of the women she had interviewed for the women's community fundraisers she had been part of, or from the TV crime shows.

She had gone to the toilet and left her drink with Joe. Could it have been the two people they had briefly chatted to? They had seemed like such a nice couple. Surely it wasn't them?

But who was this guy she had woken up next to? How had she got to the club where he said she had been and where her stuff was? And where was her partner? Would he be at her home waiting for her? Would there be a message waiting for her on her phone when she got out of here? She doubted it; the tears flowed again.

Hema arrived with the next cup of tea and a chocolate biscuit, Emmy adjusted the bed slowly so she could drink it and they all sat for a moment in silence drinking tea. The legacy of the English.

The camera clicked and flashed. Never had she ever thought she would be photographed in this area, not even in the most intimate of settings. But here she was in a sterile examination room with three other women. Three women who were doing their best to reassure her that everything would be okay. That she would heal. That she was strong. Why did she not believe any of this? How could she be okay? She had been violated. She had been left alone by the man she loved, unprotected, a man who had promised he would take care of her, give her anything she ever wanted. Promised to walk by her side, grow old with her and never hurt her.

The room was still distorting and she still felt spaced out. Her body ached, shooting pains seared through her and she felt as though she was numb and floating, but not a nice kind of floating. She felt as though she was lying in a squashy, marshmallow kind of cloud that was trying to swallow her up, not a nice soft hug but a deadly vine; dangerous, slowly crushing her, leaving her unable to move.

With the photos done, she looked up at Nikky. She saw the horror on Nikky's face, the strength it was taking her to cover it up. Nikky looked up, "They're all done now. You do have some injuries down there, but I am not going to know the full extent of them until I examine you internally. Are you ready to continue, or would you like some more time?"

"I just want it over and done with. I'm okay, let's just get it over with," she replied, knowing the more they stopped for a break, the weaker she was getting. "I still feel really strange. The room keeps distorting."

"That will be the drugs still in your system. These feelings will pass, I promise." Nikky walked over to the area her and Emmy had been documenting all the results from the examinations.

Emmy joined her, leaving Hema to the comforting role. Whispered conversations between them, with looks of concern. Both had seen these kinds of images before, seen the markings and knew that it was more than just one guy. There was no other answer for the bruising and the internal damage, and that was before the full internal had been done.

Emmy dropped her head. Sadness overtook her. How could men be so volatile? The question that always returned to her, even after having done this work for years, was *Why do men enjoy drugging a woman, or get her so drunk just to sleep with them? Why?* She, of course, knew the answers: control, fear of rejection. But she still couldn't square it in her mind. Looking over at their latest case, comforted by Hema, she forced a smile. This was one case she would remember. Such a beautiful, strong woman; violated, in such an awful way. Why was there no one to protect her? To help her. There must have been someone who saw something that could put these monsters away. But with so many victims such as this one, with nothing to remember, there was nothing to report; so, the bastards got away with it. Again.

Both Nikky and Emmy walked back over to where Hema was comforting their latest victim, they explained what was to happen and again asked permission to continue.

"Please, I've given you my permission! Please just do what you have to do!" Almost pleading, but with an air of assertion, the victim lay there, ready, or as ready as could be, for the latest intrusion into her body.

They were the longest four hours of her life. Never before had anyone looked at her in so much detail and so intimately; even though it was the least intimate experience she had ever gone through. She was glad it was over, for now. She still had the medical examination to go through, as if the forensics weren't bad enough. She would have to go through another few hours of examinations, retelling what had happened, or at least what she remembered.

Going through what had happened so Nikky and Emmy could get as much detail as possible had been awful. She hadn't been able to remember much other than the before and after. Everything in the middle was still a blank. Would having to retell it again to the doctors at the hospital bring any more of it back? Would it slowly come back to her in time? Or would it be a deep dark secret that her brain would protect her from forever? She didn't want to remember. She didn't want to relive any of it. She didn't want to know how she had come to have so much pain, so many bruises. She had told Nikky she didn't want to know any of the results either, unless it meant the need for medication to prevent goodness knows what kind of disease that had been passed onto her.

Nikky told her the doctors would be the ones to detect any infections or diseases that had been passed on, if any. She also apologised that she would have to spend more time being examined by strangers. As if it wasn't bad enough that she had gone through whatever nasty ordeal in the first place, she now had to spend hours going through examination after examination. It was a violation after violation.

Moana knew she was friendly, and some guys took that to mean that she was flirting with them, when in fact she didn't even know how to flirt. She kept going over in her mind if she wasn't so friendly to people, maybe this wouldn't have happened. She still felt dirty, ashamed and she still found it painful to move about. What had they done to her? NO! She didn't want to know! She vowed never to ask that question again simply because it may unlock the answer and she just didn't want to know.

Moana told Nikky and Emmy she didn't want to get the police involved. She couldn't remember anything, so what was the point? Going to the police and getting them to go to the place she had woken up in, describing the man who had helped her, would only cause suspicion upon him. What if he had simply been a good Samaritan? Although, how could he be? She had woken up beside him without her underwear and skirt on. He'd had sex with her, even though he told her she hadn't been able to tell him where she lived. He had taken advantage of her. Had he been the one all along? Was she protecting the very man who had violated her?

But what could she do? Without any memory, she couldn't say what had happened. She didn't even know if she had been willing, but she knew deep down the injuries and the fog that had enveloped her mind was not the result of willing participation.

A thought suddenly occurred to her… what if she had been filmed? Oh my God! What if they had filmed what had happened? She burst into tears, a new kind of fear rising up within her. She didn't know anything, other than she would not have consented to being filmed, of being with more than one guy, of being with this guy, or anyone else. She had a partner and although things hadn't been great between them, she still wouldn't cheat on him. She was a one-man woman.

Her mind wandered back to the ugly possibility that maybe, just maybe she had been filmed. Worse still, filmed enjoying it. Nausea filled her body and she could taste the bile within her stomach rising up at the back of her throat. There was no way she had been a willing participant, no way on earth. She had been raised better than that. She did not sleep around, and she had been raised that whatever happens between two people, stays between them.

But what if it turned up on a social media platform somewhere? She panicked. This could destroy her career. It would definitely destroy her parents. She started crying. She couldn't imagine how her mother would feel if she knew… or her father. She couldn't confide in anyone else; she couldn't reach out for help. She was on her own. Her head started spinning. A cold sweat broke out over her, the acidic taste of bile filled her mouth and before she knew it, she vomited everywhere.

Hema had been waiting for her to be sick, if the truth be told, and was somewhat relieved that the fear had risen up inside of this beautiful young lady and released itself. "Don't you worry about that; I'll get that cleaned up," she said handing over a bottle of water. "You have to remain strong and positive, and you also need to release all these emotions. Be kind to yourself sweetheart. Don't punish yourself or lay any blame on yourself. I can see you having those doubts, questioning yourself and your own actions, but trust me, what has happened to you is NOT your fault. If doesn't matter how friendly you are, how attractive you are, whatever you are wearing, none of this is your fault."

She knew what Hema had said was, in theory, what she would have said to a friend. But now it was her in this situation, why did she not believe these words? She had to stay strong though. She needed to be strong, to be able to smile, to pull herself out of the darkness she was feeling. She had to release her emotions, she had to allow tears to fall, she had to stop blaming herself for something she couldn't even remember happening, otherwise this would eat her up inside and destroy who she loved to be: happy, contented, and positive. That was who she was, and that would be who she would remain. No matter how long it took her to get to that place, she would get there, and she would laugh again.

Other than those who already knew, no one else would know, no one else would suspect. She would put on a brave face and become the warrior woman her grandmother had always told her she was.

SIX

THE HOSPITAL

As she sat in the waiting room of the hospital, she looked around at all the people in there. She was surrounded by people much younger than her, many looking like they were in their mid to late teens, and 'living out loud' on one of the nearest council estates. She wondered why they were there, and there alone. Where were their parents? Why were they not with them? But how could she ask that question now after what had just happened to her? Where had she been when her kids were tucked up in bed?

Feelings of fear, anger, shame, guilt, disappointment were only the tip of the iceberg. Confusion laced between them all, binding them together. How had she got there? Who was that guy? And why could she not remember? She had an excellent memory, something she had been known for. Yes, the forensics team said it was the drugs she had been spiked with, but really? They had wiped out her entire memory? Or was it the trauma of it all? The not wanting to know? How had she been given the drug? Or drugs? And were these children surrounding her playing with these drugs as a form of recreation, like she had played with Base back in her youth?

He was sat beside her, for what use he was. Sat staring into his phone yet again, saying nothing, and yet his silence and attitude said everything. "I really want a coffee. Would you mind going and getting me one, please?" she asked him. "There's a coffee shop next door on the main road."

He couldn't get out of his chair fast enough, and the moment he was gone, he took the vacuum of air with him. It was obvious he didn't want to be there, but then again neither did she. Nikky and Emmy had told her she would have to go through more examinations and go over what had happened that night all over again with the doctor. They were not allowed to share the data with anyone other than the police, and then only if the victim said they could; and only with the doctors if there was a court order.

Looking around her she noticed a couple of others who were not much older than her. Looking at them they didn't look like they'd had an easy life, but then again, looking at herself after a few sleepless nights and still in the after effects of whatever it was in her system, she was no oil painting. What else did they do here to attract this kind of patient? She got up, still in pain and walked over to a leaflet display, casually looking through them, as you would a magazine.

Pop music was playing in the background, the repetitive shallow pop music that had become so common these days. She thought about the music they played on the radio, and how people were being programmed by the amount of times certain songs were played, and how she hated the manipulation and lack of depth to it all. What had happened to the greats? What had happened to all the powerful song writers and voices? The ones who wrote songs that made a real difference in the world, rather than just adding to the white noise of teeny bopper first love, instead of the love songs of Ben E. King, or Otis Redding, the old-time greats. Aretha Franklin, a powerhouse of energy, one that stood for something, a woman who was not afraid to be all woman, a woman who inspired five generations of women, and would go on to inspire for generations to come. The closest they had to Aretha these days was Beyoncé and she still didn't come close.

She smiled to herself. For the first time since it had happened, she was thinking like her old self again, rather than in the darkness that had engulfed her. She felt a surge of positivity through her heart. She could rise from this. She could do what she always does and take something negative and make something positive from it.

He'd been gone ages getting her coffee. Had he gone to Guatemala to get the bloody beans or what? She couldn't even bring herself to think his name, let alone voice it. A surge of anger rose up within her. How could he have disappeared that night? How could he have just left her? Why had he not made sure she had got home safely? And why was he found in a shop doorway with blood all over him? Who's blood? Would there be a police officer knocking on her front door at home any minute asking to speak with him? Something she dreaded. And she knew the answers to all these questions, except the last one. Alcohol. He was an alcoholic, using the alcohol to numb the pain of his past, rather than facing up to it and loving himself. Yes, he had the physical strength, but finding the strength within himself to rise up to be the man she knew he could be, that required a different kind of strength. The love he said he had for her, showed her in glimpses, in his actions, his looks, but he didn't protect her, or them and their future. She had been right to end it.

If only she hadn't gone to see him that night. If only she had just continued to walk away from him. There were so many 'if onlys' she could come up with, but if he couldn't give up the alcohol dependency now, after this, then nothing would make him give it up. He had lost her for good now, and that broke her heart. She had believed in him, in a future together, but that could never be, not now, not ever.

She heard her name, which snapped her out of the thoughts racing through her mind. It was another woman, thank goodness for that! She put the leaflet she hadn't even read back in the rack and made her way to another examination room.

He still wasn't back with her coffee, and no doubt he would have a good excuse. He always did.

Giving the doctor her details was like talking to a robot. She had seen more warmth in the visit to the Medico Legal Centre a few years back. Had this woman become so immune to these stories that she had become as cold as a morgue to protect herself, or did she just not care?

Repeating the story over again wasn't getting any easier. In fact, it was getting more frustrating because she so desperately wanted to remember, but she didn't. She didn't want to know what had happened and was so grateful to her mind for closing off access to her for whatever reason it wanted to so she could protect herself from herself, from her memories.

There was a knock at the door. It was him, with her coffee, and an annoyed look on his face as if to say the words that then fell out of his mouth, "I've been looking for you. Here's your coffee."

In front of others he was kind and loving.

"Did you want me to stay with you or wait in the waiting room?" he asked.

"I'd rather you waited in the waiting room," answered the doctor before Moana had a chance to answer. He disappeared with a look of relief on his face. Her natural true self was understanding. It couldn't be a nice feeling knowing what had happened, especially to the woman you say you love. Knowing as a man you hadn't protected her, made sure she was home safe. How could he process this? What was it bringing up for him? Were there memories of his past surfacing that she knew nothing about? She didn't know, and at this point in time, she didn't want to know.

As she was explaining what had happened on the night in question, she kept being taken back to the moment outside when he had kissed her. The confusion, the head spinning, the numbness of her body, and the way her legs felt weak. Had it been the kiss, or the whisper in her ear? Or had he put something in her drink? The question was lingering in her mind, especially when she saw the look on the faces of the five people who now knew what had happened. They had all had the same look, especially the two forensics and the doctor who was now sat opposite her.

She spent the next hour going through what she could remember, where she hurt, how she felt before her memory loss, and how she had felt since. The doctor explained to her what she would be doing and asked her to get undressed and put on the gown which was laying on the examination table.

She needed another coffee, and the doctor kindly phoned through the reception to ask for a coffee and some biscuits. Shortly after both refreshments arrived, which give the doctor a chance to go through the notes she had made, and cross reference with the referral notes sent over by Nikky and Emmy.

"I just want you to know, these notes sent over by the team at the rape crisis centre are not complete, for confidentiality reasons. So much of what I am about to do, may already have been done. It is for your protection that we do not share these notes with each other. Do you understand?"

Something inside of Moana snapped. "Yes, I do understand. I am not one of the illiterates you no doubt often see in here on a daily basis, who doesn't care about getting 'the clap'. I am done with you treating me like some kind of slag who simply sleeps around and then calls rape just because it is convenient. I don't know why you do this job, maybe it is the science of it all that interests you, but you are one of the coldest women I have ever met, and this is not a walk in the fucking park for me."

The doctor looked shocked, as if the verbal slap in the face had been a slap across a wet face, stinging in all the places a slap could hurt. "I am sorry if I have come across as uncaring. It is not an easy job as I am sure you are aware. Seeing this day in day out, knowing how often this kind of thing happens and how many more go unreported, is challenging. I try to remain neutral, some patients don't like soft nurturing, or overly friendly, and I have to remain impartial, because if this goes to court, then I have to remain neutral. I will go and see where your coffee is whilst you put on your gown. Excuse me." And with that the doctor left the room.

Moana stood there for a moment, recovering from the pain of standing up, knowing the pain was going to shoot through her again as she tried to undress and put on the gown.

She had been so caught up in her own pain and confusion and hadn't really considered the pain and confusion these doctors must see in a week, let alone their medical career. Some women cry rape falsely, some never report it, some remember every scary moment and others, like herself, who only have the before and after. How many women out there were there? How many were so afraid they couldn't speak up? And what about the men? The boys? No doubt one of the biggest numbers of them all, too ashamed to admit it had happened to them, because not only was it traumatic but being sodomised against your will? Anal sex wasn't even talked about in the mainstream as an act between loved ones, so to admit you had been raped up the arse was a whole new conversation the world was not ready for. Her mind wandered. Just how many people were out there? And how many people from different walks of life, and how many angles did this kind of trauma have on humanity as a whole?

She was still struggling to get dressed when the doctor came back a few minutes later, with a nurse to accompany her during the examination. Introductions were made, explanations given and more forms placed on the table for Moana's consent to be given to another person being present, and for certain procedures to be done.

"Here is your coffee. Would you like some help there? Let me help you get this gown over you, then I will help you lay on the bed." It seemed like a different person had walked back into the room than the woman who had left just a few moments before. Moana noticed the doctor's eyes looked like they had been crying. "I am sorry for the way I spoke to you before. I didn't mean to be so rude or insulting," said Moana softy.

"Not at all, you were right to say what you said. This is not just my job, this is your life, something you will have to live with forever. I am sorry to say, but it does become 'just another case number' to me, but I can see this is not going to be just another case, just by reading your referral notes and the way your body is in such pain. I need you to get up on the bed, with your knees up, which I can see will be difficult for you."

Although the doctor had softened, this was such a vast difference to the three ladies she had spent four hours with the previous day. Laying on the bed, the emotions overcame her again, knowing what was about to happen, but this time she was on her own. No one to hold her hand, no one to reassure her, just a doctor who simply had a job to do.

Moana had paid attention to Nikky's face the day before when she had started the examination and did the same again with this doctor. The look of shock on the doctor's 'neutral' face said all it needed to say, and more. Would she ever know the reason for the looks of shock, and why the demeanour of both Nikky and Emmy, and this doctor changed the moment they looked at the most sacred part of Moana's body?

Did she even want to know?

No, she didn't think she did.

The tears fell from Moana's eyes, and she fell into a moment of weakness, a moment of being a victim.

Would she ever be able to shake it off?

Or would it always be there?

SEVEN

THE MEMORIES OF SPAIN

Lying there as the doctor examined her, she tried to take her mind elsewhere, away from it all, but with each touch, each movement the pain brought her back into her body. "I'm really sorry this is hurting you. I am doing my best to not hurt you, but I now need to go in deeper, and this will hurt. I am so sorry. Do you want to take a break?" the doctor asked.

The nurse had hold of Moana's hand, and was stroking her hair back off her face. "No, I just want you to get on with it so I can go home."

"Okay then," answered the doctor, as she explained what she was about to do, "I will count down slowly... 3... 2... 1...."

The pain shot up through Moana like nothing she had experienced, tears and a silent scream and then a guttural roar filled the room. The doctor apologised for the pain, but explained the necessity of needing to take swabs and photos of the damage deep inside of her... just in case they ever found the people responsible; because they knew now it wasn't just one person, there had been at least two. The semen samples and pubic hairs had proven that, along with the bruises on her ankles, wrists, and biceps.

Her eyes rolled to the back of her head and her breathing became erratic, but looking back down on her own body, at the doctor examining her, whilst the nurse held her hand, Moana didn't feel a thing. A sensation of serenity passed over her. There was no sound, no heaviness, just a feeling of weightlessness. She began to hear her own heartbeat, the muffled sound of the doctor as though either she or Moana were under water. The room was bathed in a bright white light and what could only be described as silver raindrops and white orbs. The weightlessness continued as Moana floated back towards her body, stopping just half a metre above herself lying there on the examination bed, couch, table whatever it was called. So many words, so many phrases, terms and implements flooding her mind and yet falling away as soon as they landed. There was nothing to hold onto and yet everything to retain.

"You will heal from this. You will heal more than just yourself. You will become stronger and more resilient than ever before." Words gently spoken in this ethereal place by the soul of Moana who floated about the physical self.

She could feel the warmth of her tears rolling out of the corner of her eyes into her hairline, but now there was a serenity, and a calming energy in the room. Even the nurse was smiling differently, and the doctor was looking calmer. Whatever had happened in the room just then had impacted the three of them in ways none of them would ever speak of together.

Lying there with her ankles to her hips, legs open to each side, Moana traced back the events of her life since meeting him. The first week had been amazing, filled with fun, deep laughter and memories being made and remembered. They had known each other a long time. Then a week in, things had gone bad, external forces getting in the way of each and every area of her life and putting a huge strain on them both. He had stood by her all the way through it, and just three months after getting together, they chose to meet up again in Cadiz. She was on holiday with a friend on the other side of Andalucía, whilst he was stationed in a port just up from the town of Cadiz itself. She had made her way to him on the overnight bus, and as the bus pulled up and she saw him sat there waiting for her, her heart had skipped a beat. He looked pleased to see her, and as she walked down off the bus, he wrapped those strong arms of his around her, kissed her firmly on the lips and welcomed her by taking her bag and slinging it across his shoulder. She had felt turned on in those moments and couldn't wait to be alone with him.

Making their way to the hotel they were staying in, a place she had chosen for them, they laughed, held hands, and chatted non-stop. The talking, laughing and playfulness didn't stop, until that night. The night they had gone to the flamenco show, the night she had staggered back to the hotel alone, sand in her hair, belt and watch missing and her clothes dishevelled; him nowhere to be seen or found.

She found her way back to the hotel thanks to the help of two guys who had seen her clutching her cardigan tight around her front, freezing cold, making no sense at all.

They had offered to call the police, but she just wanted to shower and get into bed, and maybe he was back at the hotel. Maybe he was waiting for her, having noticed she was gone, and thought it was best to go back to the hotel. He wasn't there. She took off her clothes, showered and got into bed, pulling the duvet up close around her, and cried herself to sleep.

She didn't know how long she had been sleeping for, but she froze as he climbed into bed, drunk, smelling of cigarettes and giggling away to himself, trying to snuggle up to her. Her body rock solid, like a piece of ice, pulling away from him.

"What's up with you? For fuck's sake! Only wanted a cuddle." He rolled over, turning his back to her and fell asleep almost immediately.

She lay there, her mind turning over and wondering what to do. No memory of what had happened. One moment she was sat opposite him eating a delicious meal, listening to, and watching the flamenco show, and the next she's staggering through the beautiful port city of Cadiz, alone, in the middle of the night.

The following morning, he refused to kiss her until he had showered and cleaned his teeth. "Man you would have loved the tunes last night! You should have heard it! And I was lifted up on the stage and was crowd surfing! Brilliant night!" he said between brushing and spitting in the sink.

Confusion was filling her mind, frown filling her face, her jaw tightening. "What do you mean? What club?"

"Oh, well after you fell over and banged your head on the cobbles, I went to get a taxi, but you were gone when I got back. I thought you had come back here and on the way back I heard this club night, so I went there. Thought you might have gone in. Obviously not as I couldn't see you, and by the miserable look on your face." He walked into the main part of their room with a towel wrapped around his lower body, rubbing his hair with the hand towel before throwing it on the floor of the bathroom ready for the maids to take it away.

"Where did you go anyway?" he asked.

"I don't know. All I remember is an older guy trying to kiss me, his breath smelling really bad, a rubbish cart and high vis jacket, walking through the streets trying to find my way back here, and calling your name. Two young guys helped me find my way back, and when I got back here, you weren't here. And my watch and belt are gone, I don't know where, or how, or why."

He stood there in his towel and just looked at her. Made no move towards her, no softening of his face, or warmth. "Do you want to talk about it? Or shall we go and get some breakfast?"

Not even listening for a response, he grabbed a fresh pair of jeans and a t-shirt. "You were pretty out of it after you banged your head to be honest. A couple of the other dinner guests asked if we wanted a lift back to the hotel, but we said we'd get a taxi, and like I said, I went looking for one and by the time I got back, you were gone. Thought you had come back here, and then that's when I came across the tunes pumping out of the club. Honestly, you would have loved it."

Why had she stayed with him? Why had she not walked away at the end of that holiday? Why? So many whys were now filling her mind. She knew why. She needed him. She wanted to be wanted. Wanted someone to love her, and because she wanted to believe it was just his way of coping with the realisation of what had happened. A common response to traumatic events that have happened to us or those we love. Avoidance. He was avoiding it, making light of it so the seriousness of what had happened, or possibly happened didn't become the reality.

The thing he was avoiding though was responsibility, responsibility of caring for the woman who was sat before him. Responsibility of a grown man, responsibility of a partner. Avoiding responsibility of his own actions of leaving her alone in a strange town having just bumped her head on a hard-cobbled street. A pattern she would see emerge even more over time and be blind to. But isn't that what love is, blind?

Over breakfast he asked her if she wanted to talk about what had happened "There's no point. I can't remember anything really, just flashbacks. And the smell of his breath." A tear rolled down her face just as breakfast was served. Suck it up, push it down, smile up at the waiter and say thank you. Modus Operandi from here on in, for the foreseeable future.

It was the last it was ever spoken of, and her oversized Chanel's were now a permanent fixture on her face. Too dark for him to see her eyes, and the tears, the doubts and the thoughts going through her mind.

She just wanted holding, and she didn't want whatever had happened to be the last time a man was inside of her.

So they fucked, had sex, made love, and cuddled, putting the past behind them. It couldn't be changed, and it wasn't him that did it to her, so best give him the benefit of the doubt. Move on. Move forward. Smile on face and focus on the road ahead. Things could only get better, because they couldn't get any bloody worse!

Horse riding hurt, but the vineyard was lovely. Meals out were great, and they were becoming known by the locals. The rest of the holiday was great, and she surprised herself with how well she had pushed that night so far out of her memory. Saying goodbye to him at the train station back to the airport was hard, and when she saw him mouth the words "I love you" to her from the platform, her heart hurt. When would she see him again? She felt a tugging in her womb, butterflies in her tummy and an ache in her heart, and then a pain shoot up her cervix…

And she was transported back into the hospital room with the doctor and the nurse still mid examination and the nurse asking her if she was okay.

No, she wasn't okay. She was far from okay, and now she was angry with herself for having stayed with him after Spain. She should have left, she should have walked away, she should have blocked him and everything about him from her life.

But she couldn't, and she wouldn't. He had her caught hook, line, and sinker.

EIGHT
THE DENIAL

Home after the examination, she was relieved Abdu had taken the boys back to his place. She could just sleep, hide under the duvet, cry, and process. But she couldn't sleep, couldn't rest, and couldn't cry. It felt like she was all out of tears, and lying down in bed just felt lazy.

She had already missed two days of building her business, and reports she had to work on for the school and up and coming court case. There was no more time to waste, not that it had been wasted, although she had. The cocktail of drugs that had been pumped into her body causing all the symptoms she was showing were untraceable, although it was clear to the doctors and the forensics team there had been a cocktail of drugs used for the aftereffects to be present, and the amount of damage that had been done to her.

They had both told Moana the extent of her damage and prescribed a variety of drugs to take to prevent sexually transmitted diseases and HIV. She would have to take anti-HIV drugs for the next month, they might make her feel a bit drowsy, but it was essential she took them at the same time every day. She was lucky there was no sign of a sexually transmitted disease so far, but again it was essential she took the different drugs to prevent any from appearing and to help fight the infections that may occur deep inside of her.

Being told it would take a week or two for the bruising on her insides to heal gave her a reality check, especially as she was about to prepare for her next grading in mixed martial arts. Still, it would give her time to be by herself and walk the dogs out in the woodlands around her home.

She was still very much in a daze and now she couldn't tell if it was the aftereffects of the cocktail of drugs she had been given, the shock the doctor advised her would start to settle in or the new drugs she had collected at the hospital.

Hearing her name called by the pharmacist, and then the prescription read out for everyone to hear, Moana could have killed the pharmacist with a look of knives. How bloody insensitive! Were the pharmacists that ignorant? Did they not give a crap about patient confidentiality? And who were they to look at her with a look of disgust on their faces, knowing what the combination of drugs were which they were handing out?

Moana felt even more shame and embarrassment in that moment, and the warmth of the tears pricked the back of her eyes. They would not show, they would not fall, and she would walk out of that hospital pharmacy waiting room with as much dignity as she could muster. The pharmacist looked shocked at Moana's reaction and sting in the thank you, not to mention the firm grip she had taken her medication with. Not quite a snatch but most definitely a force which conveyed the upset and anger Moana was feeling. Moana looked back at the senior pharmacist behind the counter, noticed he was looking at her, and the way he dropped his head she knew he knew she was pissed with his colleague.

The doctor, Nikky and Emmy had told her that she had nothing to be ashamed of, nothing to feel guilty about, but it was easy for them to say, they were not the one being treated like a leper and a cheap slut by a complete stranger who counted pills and bottled them all day.

Being a victim and referred to as a victim wasn't sitting well with Moana. She had never been a victim, would never be a victim, so it was time to put her game face on, get some rest and focus on the work at hand. She had two boys she was leading, and she had until they came home from school on Monday to get herself in the zone. Gentle walks with the dogs, lots of rest and plenty of detoxing and hot baths with meditation music, raising her frequency and recalibrating her energy levels. This healing was more than just taking the pharmaceuticals and having a therapy session, this was about a full recalibration of her energetic field.

She wasn't quite sure what the science was behind it and how it all worked, but she knew enough to know that the lower her mood the lower her frequency. If she wanted to heal, she had to be high energy, high frequency, happy and positive. She had to get grateful for everything in her life and learn to look at what she could be grateful for in this situation. She had to look for the positives in the negatives and learn from them, because this was all about the learning, the growth, the healing, and the protection of herself moving forward.

He had run her a bath – told her he would make dinner and make her a cup of tea – and she should just go and rest in the water. It was one of her favourite things to do and it would make her feel better. Whatever he had been processing over the last few days, it was making him more attentive. She liked it. He had been distant over the last 18 months, ever since they had returned from Italy, their second holiday together, but now he was doing the hoovering and preparing meals.

The downside was he was not getting along with her boys any longer. They stood up to him, they challenged him, and he didn't like it. He blamed them for trying to come between him and Moana, even though it was the amount of time he was spending with the two guys she had introduced him to. The three men had formed a strong bond and were working hard on a couple of different projects. It wasn't that which bothered Moana, it was the way he would spring up out of bed in the morning the moment one of the guys called, the late hour he would come back, having spent a couple of hours down the pub drinking and then come back, have a bath or a shower, expect food to be ready and then hide in her room watching TV programmes on his laptop. He had started using her place as a doss house, a convenience, and contributed nothing in return other than a few veggies here and there.

Why had she allowed him back? Why had she stayed with him all this time? What hold did he have over her?

Why did she need or want him to be with her? Why would she rather have him than be alone?

All these questions flying around in her head, and yet she had been in doubt ever since their holiday to Spain. She hadn't learnt then, and it didn't seem as though she had learnt now, because if she had, why was he lying in bed next to her every night even after he had left her and not made sure she had gotten home safely the week before?

Lying there in the bath Moana thought back to all the incidences in which the bad stuff happened when he was around, and the lack of memory she had over what had happened just a few days ago, and what had happened in Spain. She knew there was a reason she didn't remember, but she was interested in the pattern that had emerged with him.

She knew they had been drinking – but not a lot – maybe a bottle of wine between them over dinner, maybe two bottles over the course of five hours. Was that a lot? I mean that was, what, four or five glasses in total. She would have a glass as they looked over the menu or cooked the dinner, then another glass with the starter and main, with another as the main ended and the dessert came out, and one to round the meal off with. He would drink more, and if there was some left, they would take the bottle home, or if they were at home it would be drunk into the early hours of the morning or saved for when she relaxed in the bath with a good book.

She'd checked in with friends and they drank pretty much the same as her. Some drank more, some told her she worried too much, but she was beginning to see that whenever she went out for a meal with him, and she drank alcohol, she would lose her memory and something bad would happen.

She had known in Spain she'd had sex but had no memory of it. She knew the moment she had woken up a few days ago in that grotty flat she had had sex, painful sex, but again, no memory of it.

She was always careful. She never left her drink unattended. She had read about too many cases of this for her to be foolish. The only time she had left her drinks unattended was when she had left them on the table with him whilst she had been to the toilet. Had he taken his eyes off her drink for someone else to drop something in it? Had he put something in the drink himself hoping for a bit of action; even though that would be pointless as she would have made love to him for hours.

Her mind hurt from replaying over every detail of the evening. There had been a couple sat at the table opposite them. Had they put something in her drink when she had gone to the toilet? What did they have to gain by doing that?

The psychology of it all intrigued her, especially as she never remembered feeling drunk. She would have memories of having a good time, of laughing, but then she would always wake up with no memory. She had heard of this happening to people who drank a lot, but she was a single mum and in the process of building a business, she couldn't drink a lot, didn't drink a lot. She didn't like feeling out of control, rather always the one in control. So what was different about this, and Spain, and then Italy?

Was it the alcohol? Nikky and the doctor didn't believe it

was. Her symptoms and injuries meant there were some kind of painkillers in her system. Ketamine had been mentioned due to the amount of damage done on the inside, but with the bruising on her wrists, biceps, and ankles, it was unlikely as ketamine would have made her unable to move. The date rape drugs Rohypnol and hydroxybutyric, also known as 'roofie' and GHB, were more common and it was more likely to have been them due to the lack of drugs found in her body.

The alcohol levels were also non-existent so this was another sign it hadn't been too much alcohol, because for the memory loss and the amount of bruising to have occurred there would still be quite high levels of alcohol in her system when Nikky and Emmy did their tests. It didn't really matter which had been used to be honest, as none of them were traceable in her bloodstream. It was likely it had been GHB due to the seizure like symptoms she had described such as the eye rolling and the shaking, not to mention the depth perception being totally off. Exploring all these new pieces of information and understanding what went on inside her body was raising so many questions, and not providing enough answers.

Was she really spiked each time? Was that just too convenient an excuse? Did she get drunk incredibly easy, and her 'inner slut' just came out to play? What else did she do during these blackouts? Did she take drugs? Were there men and women in the bed? If so, how many? Was she filmed? The answers to these questions scared her. She wasn't the kind of person to perform for the camera and had never had a sexual encounter with a woman. She was a one-man woman and hadn't done drugs for a very long time. She couldn't, she was a mother now, she had responsibilities.

Was she intrigued about expanding her sexual experiences? Absolutely, but not unless it was in a safe, conscious, and loving, respectful relationship with a man she trusted. Her mind was whirring and the more answers she thought she had found, or discovered, the more questions they raised and the more she knew she would not rest until she had learnt more about these drugs and the effects on the mind and the body. Plus she was a mum of two boys, they were growing up in this world of date rape and she wanted to make sure they were aware of the challenges they may face if they said no to a girl or was in the wrong place at the wrong time. She had grown up with girls, she had seen how spiteful they had been about the boy they fancied saying no to them and choosing a 'less popular' girl to go to the school disco with, or 'hang out up town' with. She couldn't make the choices for her boys, but she could at least make sure they were informed.

As she lay there in the bath, the questions finally starting to subside, the one thing she was grateful for was the coil. If she didn't have that inside her, God only knows what would have happened if she had gotten pregnant. She didn't believe in having a termination, she knew the embryos ended up in the MMR vaccine for a start, something she wished she had never given her boys. Would she have had the courage to have the child, or would she have had the pregnancy terminated?

The thought of having a termination upset her, but knowing the child was the result of such a violent and traumatic event such as this? Would she be able to look at the child without pain or would having a child born from rape help to heal and bring love from such a traumatic event? It didn't really matter right there in that moment because the pregnancy tests done by Nikky and the doctor had both come back negative. And if she had of been pregnant, would she have known who's it was? His or the guys who raped her?

NINE

THE ITALIAN JOB

Getting out of the bath was painful, and the drop in temperature of the water made her shiver, which in turn hurt her more. How was it possible a shiver from the cold gave her such pain inside of her body?

"Are you okay?" he asked through the door.

"Yeah, it just hurts to move still," Moana replied.

"Did you want some of those painkillers the doctor prescribed? And have you had your anti-HIV tablets yet?" he asked before adding, "Dinner is ready by the way, and I have made you a cup of tea."

"Yes, no, okay and thank you," she answered, "I won't be long, just need to dry myself and get dressed."

She didn't know what to make of what was happening. A few nights ago, they were not even together, and now here he was back in her home as though nothing had happened. She was grateful he was there, but to be honest, she would have been grateful to have any of her friends there to help. She couldn't be bothered to attempt to put on her PJs. Just lifting her leg out of the bath had sent piercing pains up inside of her, right up into her front lobe right behind the adrenal gland in her brain. What had they done to her? No. She didn't want to know. The confirmation of any of the ideas in her head, or of something she hadn't even considered was just too much knowledge, and for her, too much knowledge had never been a bad thing before.

"I thought you were getting dressed?" he said, with a look she was unable to read.

"I was, but it hurt, so I didn't bother. This towel is warm enough anyway," she replied.

They ate dinner almost in silence, when once the conversation would flow, or the silence had an undercurrent of sexual chemistry. Now there was nothing. She wasn't even feeling anything. Was that the meds she had taken at the start of dinner, even though she should have taken them an hour before food? She felt like a zombie, and hardly touched her meal. "I think I am going to go to bed, get some rest. Can you do the washing up please?" she asked as she got up from the table.

"Might as well leave it until the morning, no point washing up just a few plates. Waste of water," came his reply.

She couldn't be bothered to answer, or even do the dishes herself, which is something she would have done previously. A clean and tidy kitchen was the sign of a clean and tidy person, something they had agreed upon when they first got together. Ship shape, and everything put away, with hardly anything on the work tops. Just how she liked it, but now, it didn't bother him how her home looked, unless he was trying to make a point to her boys.

She'd been lying there dozing when she heard him on the phone to whoever it was. She could make out what was being said but not who he was saying it to. She knew he didn't want to be there, was only biding his time, and the comments he was making to whoever was on the other end of the call only added to her previous suspicion of him being with one of the women whom he'd worked with just a few months before. She'd seen a message from her one night as they were playing a word game on his phone, 'Are you awake? Is she with you?' The likelihood of Moana being with him was very high as he had been living with her during his time off, and it was also very likely that he was awake given the time of night it was. He had grown even more distant since that work trip away, a distance which had started when they were in Italy in the October of the year before.

As she lay there remembering the holiday as if it were yesterday, she smiled. She had always wanted to go to Italy, and he had surprised her with the flights. From meeting in the airport, to champagne on the flight, everything had been going great. They had moved on in leaps and bounds since their holiday in Cadiz the year before. The past was firmly behind them and they were even discussing their future plans: a property, sailing club, youth activity centre, giving back to the community. They had even talked about the different kinds of property they would need – though how they would be able to afford it on their current income levels, would be the question.

He had started looking at career progression, getting excited about what was possible, and her business plan expanded beyond anything she had thought possible. She knew she would always make more money than him, but she didn't care. He would put in more physical hard graft and save them loads of money on the building costs and maintenance moving forward. When he was away he called every opportunity he had, for an hour at least each time. He would find time for them, make time for them, and it resulted in her feeling safe in their relationship.

Driving through the Italian mountains from Puglia to Naples, they had laughed and talked constantly. This was the kind of relationship she had been looking for, the energy, the sense of adventure and the laughter. The first few days had been more than magical, but he'd blown that after they enjoyed a beautiful day out in Rome.

The day had been perfect, the Colosseum, museums, sneaky kisses, looking out across the city as the sun went down – and he had even taken her to a book shop which had first editions in it. She was mesmerised, like a child on the happiest day of their life. Touching a first edition of fairy tales, books hundreds of years old, leather bound and hidden behind glass in the cabinets that housed them.

The lady in the bookstore asked if she wanted to hold a copy of one of the books, excitedly Moana said yes. Eagerly putting on the white gloves she joked with him, "They are like queasy quaver raver gloves!" They had both laughed and it was probably one of the most magical moments she had felt. Had he planned to take her there? Or was it just happenstance? It didn't matter, in that moment, nothing mattered.

She was in her element, surrounded by some of the oldest books in European history outside of Oxford and Cambridge. Philosophy, history, the Romantics, all leather bound, paper so fragile within the covers that the smallest amount of acid from a human hand, or too heavy a touch, and the page would disintegrate before your eyes.

Not wanting to leave, but having to as the shop was closing, Moana thanked the lady and clasped her hands together in front of her face like an excited child who'd had far too much chocolate for even a grown adult. He had pulled her close and whispered how beautiful she looked when she was this happy, and how he hoped to make her even happier than she had ever been. He kissed her firmly on the lips with such passion she was taken aback, and had they not been in the busy streets of Rome, she would have made love to him right there and then.

Hungry, they started looking for a restaurant to eat dinner in, walking through the side streets away from the hustle and bustle of the main parades, they made their way to an exclusive part of town. He had led the way and told her he wanted them to have a special evening together, to round off a really great day. They found a restaurant after about an hour and were surprised at just how big the place was, considering there were about 15 tables outside, and a further 30 tables inside. Wine bottles were on every whitewashed wall, and a huge open kitchen was the centrepiece as you walked in. What with the water glasses, and a glass of wine per course – one for the fish starter, the meat main and the dessert wine – there was a constant flow of glassware on and off the table.

Remembering this night and the glass of wine per course, and the pre meal glass of wine, reminded Moana of just how normal it was to have a glass of wine with every course of the meal. She felt better about the amount they had drunk over dinner the night they had met up again just a few nights before. Her mind then wandered to the lunches she had enjoyed with her girlfriends, a glass whilst deciding what to eat, a glass whilst enjoying the main course and maybe an aperitif afterwards, depending on the day of the week and who was on the school run.

The trip to Italy soon flooded her mind again and that's when she remembered how it had all gone horribly wrong, but this time it had been at the end of his hands. Dancing away in a club they had found after finishing their meal, they had made quite an impact on the other clientele. Moana had owned the dancefloor whilst he was busy alternating between drinking and dancing with her. He told her he was going to go to the bathroom and that his bag was behind the bar with Giuseppe.

After a while she noticed he wasn't back from the toilets, and the music was dying down. Where was he? Everyone had come to know who they were, and no one had seen him for ages. She started to panic. Where was he? No one in the club knew where he was. No one had seen him in the club for at least an hour. Had that much time gone by?

Now Giuseppe and the bouncers were beginning to look concerned, when one bouncer came up to her and showed her a picture of him, lying face down on the floor. Eyes wide and fear in her heart, she asked where it was.

"One block to the left and around the back of the building."

She sprinted to find him. What was he doing outside of the club, and why would he be lying on the ground face down? She found the alley way, sprinted down into the darkness towards the light at the end of the tunnel, and as she looked to her right, there he was just as she had seen in the photo.

How had the bouncer got hold of this photo? Who had taken the photo? Why was there no-one there with him now? So many questions flying through her mind, and even now as she remembered this night over a year ago, her heart still raced.

She remembered screaming his name, his lifeless body unresponsive. She slapped his face. Nothing. Kissing his face, stroking his face, screaming his name, nothing worked. Giuseppe turned up with his bag, her scarf and a bottle of water. Giuseppe gave her the bottle of water and she took a sip so she could pour it into his mouth without spilling too much. Nothing. Not a murmur. Slapping his face again and propping him up she tried to tip the water into his mouth, which she had manged to prise open. Still nothing. She slapped his face even harder to bring him around and then poured water over his entire face. This time he murmured and so she kissed him, thanking God he was still alive.

She gave him more water, the bouncers who were still standing there, were now having to return back to the club. Giuseppe told her he had to go back to the club and make sure everything was locked up, and that he would be back shortly. She nodded her head and carried on trying to revive her man. Another splash of water should do the trick, so she poured a little more water over his forehead. Before she knew what was happening she was on her back with him kneeling on her chest, hands around her throat telling her she wasn't "so fucking clever this time bitch!"

She couldn't breathe, all she could see was the silhouette of a man in the distance over his right shoulder to her left. His grip tightening around her throat, her breathing becoming more laboured and silver rain drops pouring over the lens of her eyes, she started to feel limp. The man from the background was now stood beside Joe and they both stood there, hands on their hips laughing at her. Coughing she tried to compose herself and get to her feet. Her head spinning with the look of evil in his eyes as he had her pinned to the ground, and now the disgust he had written all over his face, mocking her as she clambered to her feet.

"That's it bitch! Get to your feet and get out of here," he shouted at her as she made her way back down the alley to the main road where the club was. She made it to the club, but it was locked, and it didn't matter how much she banged on the door, no one could hear her.

She turned and saw a taxi, it stopped and she got in and told the driver where she needed to go. She left him in the yard at the back of the club. It was over. Whoever he had just turned into, she never wanted to see him again. She knew it wasn't the man she had just spent the night with, and the last amazing few days driving around Italy. She didn't know who he was, all she knew was he had turned into someone else.

Halfway back to the hotel, she realised that she didn't have money to pay the taxi. He had it. And he had the key to the hotel room. Arriving back at the hotel, she tried to explain to the taxi driver that she had no money, as she had the door open and one leg out of the taxi. The taxi driver said he would need paying, yet showed concern. The next thing she knew he was asking her to pay him in sexual favours. She leapt out of the car and slammed the door. This was not going to happen to her again. She called him a pervert and he sped off at high speed.

Standing on the side of the road, in the early hours of the morning, she sobbed. How could this have happened again? First Cadiz, now Rome? How cursed was this relationship? She decided to try and knock on the door of their hotel, but no one answered. The hotel was small, with doors closing at 1 am. It was now past 3 am and everyone would be sleeping.

She had the key to the car, so she got into the car and made herself comfortable. "Sleeping in the fucking car! What the actual fuck?!?" The hotel had been an exclusive boutique hotel and was supposed to be a treat, but here she was in a cold car, shaking like a leaf, alone and afraid of what would now happen.

She had soon fallen asleep crying, and as the sounds of the day had started to happen she woke up and headed over to the hotel. The owner opened up the door in shock at her coming in having said goodbye to her the previous night. He looked for her partner, and then looked back at her with a concerned look on his face. She just dropped her head and gently shook it from side to side. He ushered her in and made her sit down in the reception area whilst he made her coffee and got the porter to get the spare key to her room.

There was the beautiful king size bed, not slept in and it wasn't as if she could now go to sleep as she had only booked one night, and checkout was in an hour, with every other room in the place booked up. She thanked the hotel manager as he brought her another coffee, on the house. She thanked him and used the bathroom to freshen up before leaving and making her way to the coffee shop over the road.

Pulling out her journal and her laptop, she started looking at options. What would she do now? She had the hire car, another ten days in the country before her flight home and she wanted to see Italy; nothing was going to stop her. She hadn't heard from him, there was no message and to be honest she didn't really want there to be. She sat working away in a really quiet coffee shop and was about to put things away and head to the car when she got a call from an unknown number.

Upon answering it, she was told she needed to attend the British Embassy and ask for one of the officials on duty. What on earth did the embassy want? Had they found him? Was he alive? Had he been arrested? What was she about to walk into, if indeed she went? The gentleman on the call sounded very concerned, and the fact they had her phone number concerned her. She had to go. She had no choice. This was the embassy calling.

Arriving at the embassy, the guards acted as though they were expecting her. They stepped to the side and let her in, where another guard led her into a small office to the left of the security hall. Joe was sat there, looking really fragile and dazed. A smile broke out over his face as soon as he saw her.

She didn't smile, she didn't even want to see him, and her reaction made him frown, as it did the official who was stood there to greet her.

"Signora, welcome. We are glad you came. The police

found your fiancé wandering the streets this morning looking very confused. He says that you got separated last night and was concerned for your safety. He doesn't remember much from last night, but we wanted to make sure that you were okay. Are you okay?"

"Yes, thank you. A little tired, but I am well thank you. What happens now?"

The official looked surprised that she had not addressed her fiancé and had asked where they were staying and she told them she was driving to Florence that day, stopping off on the way. She was unsure as to where she would stay.

"Ah, okay. Well, if I could ask you to sign this form to say that we have contacted you and you are free to go as you wish."

"Thank you, Sir." She signed the paperwork and Joe got up and followed her out of the building. Grabbing for her hand, she pulled away. Turning to look at him, she saw confusion sweep across his face.

"What's wrong? You seem really distant, and really upset with me."

"You could say that. And are you trying to tell me you have no idea why I may be angry and upset with you?" she said, trying to keep her voice controlled whilst they were in the vicinity of the embassy.

He said he had no idea, so she told him. She told him it was over between them, that she was going to continue with her trip, and he could do as he liked. He grabbed her by the hands, a deep sadness in his eyes, "I would never hurt you. EVER. You have to believe me."

She pulled the scarf from around her neck that she had

put there when she had showered in the morning, put there to hide the marks on her neck, which had been in plain sight of the hotel manager, who had politely not mentioned them.

"Then what do you call these?" she snapped back at him.

Confusion, fear and sadness engulfed him, either that or he was a bloody great actor. Tears filled his eyes. "I have no memory of last night, other than when we were in the restaurant enjoying ourselves and the last thing I remember is writing you that note telling you I loved you and this was the best night we've ever had and wanting every night to be like this. That is honestly the last thing I remember. Moana, I swear."

She looked at him, unable to know whether to trust him or not. She continued walking with him right beside her, trying to convince her of his innocence. Telling her he had been walking the streets looking for her all morning. That he had woken up on a park bench outside a restaurant, really cold. He asked her where his bag was, and she told him the last time she saw it was with him and the man that stood beside him as they laughed at her on the ground. It was by his feet, with his coat draped over it. That Giuseppe had brought it out to them in the back yard at the end of the alley. The look of confusion crossed his face back and forth. "Who's Giuseppe?"

"Who's Giuseppe? The man who became your best friend as you were in the club buying all the drinks for everyone telling everyone I was going to be your wife. The man who had his bouncers looking in the local area for you and who brought me your things and a bottle of water for you, just before you leapt up and pinned me to the ground almost killing me."

"Moana, I swear to you, I do not remember any of that. I would never hurt you; I love you too much to ever hurt you."

"You already have. In Spain, and now here. It's over, Joe." And with that she walked off ahead of him. He stood there in shock, and then raced ahead of her, stopping her in her tracks. "Moana, you have to believe me. I do not know what happened. I swear I don't." He was pleading with her now, before asking, "So you don't know where my bag is?"

"Nope, and I don't care either. I am going back to the café to think about things. I suggest you figure out what you want to do too."

Tears running down her face both in heartbreak and in pride for herself at having told him it was over; she made her way back to the café where she had been when she got the call from the embassy.

He walked in about ten minutes after her, and she could tell he was sorry, that he had no idea what was going on. She had never seen a man look so forlorn. He asked if he could sit with her. Part of her wanted to say no, but the biggest part of her wanted to hear what he wanted to say. So, she nodded, and he talked. Talked like she had never known him to talk. He told her he was deeply sorry, again reiterating he had no idea, and that he would never knowingly hurt her. She was the woman he wanted to marry, to spend the rest of his life with.

She told him that he had to make a choice, to either step it up and sort his shit out, and choose her over the drink, or it was over for good. This time she would forgive him, and it was up to him what he wanted to do, but either way she was going to continue with her holiday.

He told her he wanted to come with her, to be with her, and he chose her, would always choose her.

With these memories flooding her mind and the rest of the Italian holiday, up to Tuscany, across the country, their four day stay on an olive farm, they rebuilt their relationship, or so she thought. It was never the same again, especially after he stayed with his friend in London.

There were so many reasons why she should have ended it. She should have walked away after Spain, again after Italy, and again after so many of the other problems presenting themselves. Never in her life had she had such curveballs, and just in the 18 months she had been with him, her life had been turned upside down, nearly costing her access to her children, almost bankrupting her, and now this latest trauma of a gang rape and the HIV medication she was now going to have to take for the next 30 days.

If she didn't leave him after this, when would she? What would it take for her to wake up? To walk away and never be near him again?

He climbed into bed next to her, pulled her close to him and kissed her on the back of the neck. Told her he loved her and then snuggled into her.

After everything she had just remembered about their time in Italy, it was almost as if he had taken them back to an alternative ending of the night it had all gone wrong... again.

TEN

THE EXCUSES

Why had he gotten into bed and hugged her like this? He couldn't bear to be near her most of the time these days. Had refused to make love, have sex, or even fuck her since they had returned from Italy, telling her that "he'd evolved" but never explaining more to her than that. She understood perfectly well that intimacy was more than having intercourse in any of its guises, but going celibate – if that's what he was doing, without even discussing it with her – felt like he was taunting her, or punishing her. What for she had no idea, but that's what it felt like.

Was he still racked with guilt after what had happened in Italy? Unlikely, he had kind of made love to her whilst they stayed in the agritourismo olive farm in Italy. They had only meant to stay for one night but ended up staying for four nights, all at her expense considering he had lost all the cash, and his friends expensive Nikon camera, his MacBook Air and coat.

Had he not been flashing the cash in the club in Rome, maybe he would still have all of those things, but that was the thing she had learnt about him, he couldn't keep money in his hands or put money aside to invest in the future. He had to buy dinner for everyone, or buy gifts for people, or 'piss it up the wall' as he had bragged to his latest work colleague Nigel that he had a new bromance going on with.

The resentment she was feeling as she lay there, the jealousy, the stupidity, wanting it to all go away, and be replaced by the love she thought she once had for him, which she now knew wasn't love, it was intoxication. He wasn't her soul mate, he was her wound mate, and a fucking deep wound mate he was too.

She would make excuses that it was good for her to be going through this, she was learning lessons, learning how to love herself, learning how to be in a relationship that wasn't built just on sex, but a deep friendship, because let's face it when the droop gets him later in life, and old age sets in, it is going to be his personality and his big heart that will keep him attractive to her.

But that was the thing, he wasn't showing her the attention she wanted, or deserved, just telling her to stop being so needy. Whenever she questioned him, told him they had needed to talk, he had turned round and told her it was all in her head, that she was paranoid.

Sleep finally came to her, and she was awoken by her beloved dogs jumping on the bed ready for their morning walk, and him shoving them off the bed saying, "For fuck's sake!"

They needed walking, and it was obvious he wasn't going to walk them, even though he knew it was painful for her to walk. And he claimed the youngest dog was his, even though he had never walked them, or contributed to the food or vet bills.

She eased herself up into the sitting position and started to get out of bed. He just pulled the duvet up over his head and didn't say anything, making it absolutely clear he had no intention of walking the dogs or making conversation.

Painfully she got dressed, took one of the anti-HIV tablets from the bottle and then one of each of the other tablets, went to the toilet, applied the cream and washed her hands, before putting on her coat and boots, leashing the dogs and leaving the apartment.

As she walked around the back of Tesco, she decided to take a longer walk. She didn't want to be near him, his careless attitude, his dismissive comments, or his laziness. His laziness made him laugh, he was only lazy when it came to things in her home, but their friends Jo and Craig were building a fitness centre and he couldn't do enough to help them. Up and out the door the moment Craig texted or called him in the morning; a bone of contention between them, especially as when he was back from working away he was always with them, working, drinking or looking after their kids, rather than being with her and her boys.

When would she leave him? When would she wake up? When would she stop making excuses for him?

How little self-respect did she actually have that she would allow him to treat her, and her boys like this in their own home?

And the thing was, he would always have a 'good answer'. It was always her who was nagging him. Always her who was needy. Always her who was too much. Always her who couldn't 'just leave it'. Always her 'putting her head where it didn't need to be'. Always her. Never him.

He would always make sure she was reminded of the things he did behind the scenes, like reminding the boys about things, or bringing home random objects from down on the farm, or the ideas she always rejected when it came to her business.

The digs he would make about her being the big money maker, and always suggesting they go out, or order a takeaway, and then behaving like a spoilt child because he didn't get his own way, taking himself off to 'his room' to watch TV on his new MacBook Air, whilst she was at the early stages of building a business, one that was supposed to be funding their future.

Before she knew it all these thoughts had taken her on a really long walk, not that the dogs minded, they were having a great time playing with all the dogs in the woods, with her youngest dog wanting sticks thrown, especially in the water. She had become a water baby like Moana, it was hard wired into their DNA, and it didn't matter how cold or muddy it was, there was always a stick found and thrown.

She hadn't realised how far they had walked, and she wanted to get back and have something to eat. She hadn't eaten much over the last few days due to the remnants of the nausea. The days had passed by in a daze, feeling like it had happened weeks, months, years ago, until she moved, and the pain shot through her once again.

She had a lot of work to prepare for a court case she was working on, again something that had come into her life because of him. Since they had met there had been one trauma after another. A few friends had told her she was too good for him, that he didn't deserve her, that he was just using her, but she would always defend him with "you don't know him like I do", and their reply always being "I don't need to know him like you to do to know he's no good for you".

Two of the men she knew through business, Marcus whom she'd known since she was 21, and Gino who had only known her for a few years, both told her he was no good, that he was controlling her, that she should get out. Gino had been the ever loving, Italian charmer and had told her many times to leave him, to walk away. The amount of times she had sat in his restaurant and chatted, him telling her to leave him, to love herself more and dump his sorry arse and marry him instead, would make her cry and smile. He had seen through him the very first moment she had introduced them to each other, dropping his head and shaking it in a "what are you doing with him?" kind of way, only to be asked the question the very next day when she stopped by for their daily coffee together.

They were dear friends, and he would never let her pay for coffee, or lunch, even though she offered every time. He would sit and watch the horse racing, and she would sit and work away, swapping tips and choosing the next winner, agreeing they were both already winners... and then they would laugh before a solemn look would cross their faces, because winners in love neither of them were.

Walking through the door of her apartment, taking the dogs straight into the bathroom for a warm shower after their walk in the October freshness, the place felt empty. She'd left her phone behind, not even switched on as she didn't want to speak with anyone; and it wasn't until she had showered and dried the dogs, made herself a coffee and some breakfast that she realised he had either picked up her phone to check it or simply seen it and moved it.

He wasn't there, and there was no note. She knew where he had gone, and they were welcome to him. She was hurting, angry and just wanted him to have paid her even ten percent of the care and attention Abdu had when he had come to take care of her. There was no point wishing that though, Abdu was ten times the man and provider Joe was, and as tears fell down her face she wondered if she still loved Abdu, or was it just because he had shown up and been kind to her?

Was the reason she was pushing Joe away, if she was pushing him away, because she still loved Abdu? Yes, she loved him. Yes, they had healed their relationship since the betrayal and divorce, but had it really been a betrayal? Really? Or had he just been processing everything he needed to go through? Should she have stayed and made it work? Chosen to be a second wife? The thought of sharing any man with another woman, other than his mother, sisters or their daughters in a very different kind of love, was just not an appealing option for her. But did she still love him? Could she love him again?

Her mind was all over the place, she was tired again, and didn't even bother to switch on her phone. The boys were at school, and so there was no real need to turn her phone on as the school had the number for the apartment. If there was a problem, the school would phone that number. She finished her breakfast and eased herself down onto the couch, poured herself another fresh coffee, adding the best coconut milk she had found, and started reading the latest chapter on family law.

She woke up to her eldest dog pawing her arm and telling her he needed to go for a walk. How long had she been asleep? She looked at her fitness watch and realised she had slept for quite a few hours, the page only a page further on than when she had opened it. Her dog did his little growl of "come on mummy, we need the toilet" and the moment she moved the book, he was off the couch and running to the kitchen.

By the time she arrived, he had pulled his leash off the hook and dropped it at her feet. "You're such a clever, cute dog you are," she giggled, giving him a scratch under her chin. Her other dog was running round in circles with her leash too. "Did you get it yourself too? Or did Shadow get it for you? Hey Ginger?"

She didn't want to go on the same walk again, so they went the other way and did the inclined loop, she wanted to see how this walk felt with its long slight incline rather than the short steep one behind Tesco. It was slightly longer and much quieter, and the dogs had to keep to the path, and not run out into the road whilst off their leash. She saw a few familiar faces waving from their windows and from their cars, and as they came back round to the apartment she realised it wouldn't be long before the boys came home from school. They were coming home tonight, and she couldn't wait to see them. She had been deliberating on what to cook for them and chose to make them their favourite home-made fish and chips. She had all the gluten free tempura batter ingredients, the fresh fish in the freezer and the potatoes 'Because you know if you are going to have fried food you might as well have the very best and healthiest version of it, right?' Something she had said to the boys many times over.

Suddenly she stood there, a wave of realisation washing over her, like a cascade of bricks falling away around her. She was making the best of a bad lot. She was a hypocrite. Here she was working with others on how to have the best life, coaching them to be the very best version of self, living a life they loved, and here she was in a toxic narcissistic relationship, miserable, alone and putting on a brave face. No wonder she was not getting the results she wanted. She was giving out one message and living another. There was no integrity in her words, no self-love, even though she thought there had been. There was no self-respect, even though she thought that by seeing him in his highest potential, the man she thought he wanted to become, the man she knew he had the capabilities to become, he would never become that man. She had to stop believing in the potential of others and start believing in her own potential.

"Bloody fish and chips, what a metaphor," she giggled to herself. In that instant, something in her shifted. She didn't know what, but she felt it. Goosebumps rushed all over her body and she shivered, and this time it didn't hurt her inside. She just felt like she was glowing from the inside out. She couldn't explain it, she didn't even try to figure it out, she just started prepping dinner for her and her boys. She wasn't cooking for him, not anymore, not unless he made changes to his attitude and behaviour. She had to stop making excuses for him, for herself, because not only was she abusing herself, she was also showing her boys that it was okay to treat women the way he was treating her, and it wasn't far from it.

The boys asked where he was over dinner and if they were allowed to have the rest of the fish goujons. She told them to help themselves, he wasn't joining them for dinner.

He didn't arrive back at her apartment until the boys had gone to bed, her eldest walking the dog just before he went so she didn't have to. They had asked how she was feeling, and she told them she was feeling better. She was just about finished making them lunch for the next day at school when he came back through the door smelling of beer, asking her if there was any dinner left. She told him there wasn't and told him she was going to bed as soon as she'd finished the boys' lunch.

"You're not making them their lunch are you? Can't they get something at school?" he mocked in his half drunken stupor.

"Yeah, they could, but I am their mother and I want to make them something. I've been making you stuff to take to the farm with you, why not make it for the two people whom I love the most in the world?" And with that she closed the lids on the pasta salad boxes and put them in the fridge. She went through to the boys' bedroom, looked at them sleeping, kissed their foreheads and told them she was sorry, and that she loved them. Then she whispered, "Things are going to change around here from now on, I promise. You deserve better male leadership, a better life, and that is going to happen."

With that she walked out of their room, into the

bathroom and washed herself ready for bed. He had gone to sit in the room in front of his laptop and was tapping away on his phone. No change there then. "I sent you a message today," he said with an edge to his voice.

"I haven't had my phone on all day. I wanted some time to myself," she replied. "Good night."

And with that she went to bed.

He climbed in beside her, her pretending to be asleep, wondering if he would pull her to him again like he had the night before. He didn't. He just got in, pulled the duvet up over him and turned his back to her.

Hurt people hurt people. And they were both hurting, but that was no excuse.

The dogs were settled down, Shadow under the bed snoring away, and Ginger by her feet on the top of the duvet.

All of a sudden he lost his temper with Shadow's snoring and shouted, "Fucking dog, should be kept outside."

She froze in fear. She remembered Italy and the way he had attacked her in the back yard of that building behind the club. Then she thought to herself, *If he dares do anything to my dog...*

Shadow stopped snoring. Both dogs jumped up on the bed to be cuddled by her. She moved further into the middle of the bed, so both dogs could be snuggled, whilst also making sure she didn't touch him. She didn't need to worry though, he moved himself further to the other edge whilst muttering something under his breath.

The next day he told her he was going back to live with their mutual friends. She breathed a silent sigh of relief, but also felt a pain in her chest. She couldn't look at him without wanting him to kiss her, to hold her, to go back to who they were before all this crap happened; but it wasn't going to work, and she knew it deep down, she was just going through the motions.

"It will be good to have a bit of space, whilst we figure things out."

She nodded in agreement and said, "See you later then, say hi to everyone for me."

He turned to kiss her and kissed her deeply. "Let me know if you need anything. I'm only up the road."

She answered with, "I will." But she knew she wouldn't.

After he was gone, she spent time going over the last three years they had been together, the actual time they had been together, either in person or on a Skype call. She listed everything that had happened, both holidays, the court cases, the mind games, the distance, the celibacy – something he was still choosing, not giving her an answer or any explanation.

She listed all the things he did that made her feel crap, all whilst knowing that no one can make you feel crap unless you give them permission to, as Eleanor Roosevelt had once said. She listed all the things she loved about him, and nothing stacked up.

She was off on holiday with the boys soon, and to take a break just by herself. Her and the boys had discussed plans for her to do a global book tour and to live at sea, but that was years away yet, and not until her youngest had left school.

But then that night in the bath changed all that when

she was listening to a podcast by a woman she knew. She knew she couldn't continue to live life on land. This wasn't her world, her soul ached for the ocean and she needed to be free from the day-to-day to heal from all this bullshit she had just listed. She couldn't keep pushing it down, putting on a brave face, going through the motions. She needed a break; in many ways did she need a break.

Her boys deserved better, and she couldn't give them that whilst she was dealing with everything she was processing. She was snapping at them, too tired to concentrate on a conversation. Although to the outside world she was super mum, super mum was the last thing she felt like. She felt like she was letting her boys down on so many levels. She was distracted, she was distant, and she still had a lot to do to clear her name in the court room in just over a month's time – on her 40th birthday.

She had brought this man into their lives and since then there had been nothing but one shit storm after another. They needed her, not him. He was a grown man and could look after himself. He was jealous of the attention she showered on her boys, but she was their mum. She had put her own needs ahead of theirs, and now she was paying for it. When they were at school she was doing her absolute best to make sure she kept driving her business forward, collect all the data for the court case. She was coaching others and yet felt like her own life was falling apart.

Days went by and she lost track of time, how long ago was it that it happened? A week? Two? How many anti-HIV tablets did she have left to take? That would tell her. She would count them and know she was one day further away from the nightmare that still haunted her: at night; every time she stepped out at night to take the dogs for a walk; she couldn't face the ladies in the bakery next door.

And she didn't really want to see their mutual friends, friends that had been hers, and now she felt like she couldn't even be friends with them. How could they not see who he was? How could they not see the person he was? Or was it her? Was he right? Was she too needy? Was she too intense? Was what her ex-husband had said when they got divorced – that she would find it hard to find someone to love her – was that true? Was she just better off on her own?

ELEVEN
THE ABYSS

The month passed in a daze. She had good days, and she had bad days. At night she would cry herself to sleep, and she was able to pass off the fear, and the sleepless nights as a side effect of the court case. People knew about that, and it provided her with a great cover story. Her latest ally in the court case, Mr Tom, could tell straightaway the problems going on – he knew just from hearing the story of the court case the kind of background Joe had come from. It was scary, almost textbook.

"He's a manipulating narcissist, a lot of them are. I am right, aren't I? Tell me he doesn't do all of these things…" and he listed pretty much everything she had written down on the list she had made the week before, and brought her attention to so many other things which were textbook narcissism.

How could she have not seen it? One of the modules she had studied in Psychology was narcissism, and sociopath, and he was everything listed down to a letter. She had missed it all, love really was blind.

She was kept awake at night due to the nightmares of it happening again, different scenarios every time, all starting with him being with her and all ending up with her on her own, and him covered in someone else's blood, in a shop doorway. One man, two men, three men… it didn't matter really, it all ended the same way, her on her own in the forensics room, sounds of the camera clicking and flashing and the excruciating pain shooting up through her body.

Being reminded of what had happened to her every day she took the anti-HIV meds: feeling dirty, shameful, in fear of not being able to prevent herself from having HIV, and then that turning into AIDS – it made her think about all the ways you could contract HIV, and how many people around the world had it. She'd looked on Google, researched the topic, and at one point chuckled to herself as she realised that if anyone ever checked her search history they would find a really random mix of subjects.

Everything she researched for the boys, to present them with different scenarios in their schoolwork, different angles for them to consider, in different times and cultures, such as the religious rituals performed by different faiths around the world and how they had been morphed over the years, right through to the shamans and witchcraft using herbal medicines. And then going down the rabbit hole with police corruption and brutality.

But it wasn't funny, and this was now her reality. She had had more test results back. She was clear of all sexually transmitted infections, not diseases as they were once called. It was obviously more palatable for those who had contracted them previously, and oh so more socially acceptable to have an infection than a disease – or rather dis-ease.

Moana's blood tests came back, the semen didn't match anyone on police record so they couldn't tie her case to an outstanding one or another case closed. It seemed the only thing left to do now was finish the remaining days of the anti-HIV drugs.

She was literally counting down the days until she could put it all behind her, but could she? Would she ever? Only time would tell, and the time right now was telling her that she had to take better care of herself and remove him from her life. Easier said than done, especially as he was now paying her more attention, sending her more messages, calling her throughout the day to see how she was.

Maybe living apart was good for them. Maybe the time away from each other would be a great thing. Maybe he'd had the wakeup call he needed to just how lucky he was to have a woman who had put up with so much, and still welcomed him into her home, even though he contributed nothing.

That was when he turned up with a huge box of veggies, and then started sharing the cost of things, and it was strange, suspicious even. Why, all of a sudden, was he paying her this attention, paying his share of things. Was he realising what he was about to lose if he didn't step up and become the man she believed he could be? Was he wanting to make her potentially last days of freedom better? The court case was just a couple of weeks away and so was her birthday party. She would be going to the court by herself, giving her two days after she got back before her and her children would be going on their holiday, and for Moana she had now extended her time abroad to a six month trip. And if it all went well, a trip around the world.

With the trip coming up, Abdu had agreed to move into her apartment. It was the most logical thing to do financially, and for the boys. It would make the handover of duties smoother, giving them time to make sure everything was ticked off on the well thought out list Moana had made. They had been getting on really well, and now Joe wasn't living there anymore, it just made sense.

She battled every day with the thought of leaving her boys, but she knew she was no good to them whilst she was processing everything that was going on. She was exhausted from the court case, exhausted from the sleepless nights due to the nightmares, exhausted from just feeling like she was treading water all the time.

If she wasn't having a sleepless night imagining herself being taken away to prison in the court room, and not seeing her family for a few years, then she was scared she would wake up to the old man's smelly breath in Spain, or Joe's hands around her throat and the look of pure evil in his eyes, or waking up in the grotty shit hole she had woken up in just a few weeks earlier.

He stayed over one night and in the middle of the night, about 3 am, just after she finished the anti-HIV meds, she screamed out in pain. She couldn't breathe. At first she thought it was him with his hands around her throat, but then realised she felt as though she had been winded. He was, of course, annoyed with her for having woken him up, but she couldn't breathe, and he soon started rubbing her back and reassuring her, asking her where it hurt, what she was feeling.

All she could say was, "I think I have a trapped nerve in my neck."

She tried laying down again. It was only 3:30 am now and she wanted to go back to sleep, needed to go back to sleep. A fitful, painful rest of the early morning sleep she had, and the pain was still there hours later. She called the chiropractor as soon as they were open and booked an emergency appointment. It would be a different chiropractor to her usual one, the practice manager was on holiday. But it didn't matter, she needed to see a chiropractor.

Lots of questions, very little back and neck cracking and a refusal to treat her more than the odd slight adjustment, the chiropractor told her to go to the hospital. He didn't like the sound of things. She was confused, why would she need the hospital, all she needed was an adjustment.

Moana left the chiropractic centre and headed to the tram stop. She got there just in time to board the tram so she could meet her son for pizza at their favourite pizza place. She pulled out her phone and did as she was told for once, she called the hospital line. Explaining what had happened the woman sat opposite her looked up and urged her to go to the hospital. She was an off-duty nurse and felt it was essential she went – it sounded as though there was either blood clots on her lungs or on her heart.

With this news she panicked. She was flying to the other side of the world with her boys in a couple of weeks, she couldn't have blood clots on her heart or her lungs! Plus, she was meeting her youngest son for pizza, she didn't have time for the hospital.

The man on the other end of the phone told her that she had to get off the tram and he was sending an ambulance to meet her. He started tracking the tram she was on and co-ordinating the ambulance. Within moments of her getting off the tram there was the ambulance. She was helped into the back, asked to lay down and within moments she was hooked up to heart monitors, had the finger pulse reader attached to her finger, all her details were checked, and the ambulance crew were calling ahead to the hospital. It all sounded so surreal, she started feeling faint.

Was it the rush of adrenaline? It must be, she felt fine otherwise, except she didn't really. She was exhausted and this was just too much for her. She closed her eyes, but the paramedic said her eyes were rolling into the back of her head, and here she was having another one of those out of body experiences she'd had in the forensics room with Nikky and Emmy. Was this her soul's way of getting her to get present to what had happened to her, what was happening to her? Like her mum used to say "take a bloody good look in the mirror before they start pointing the finger" whether she was talking about a bully on the news, or someone who she heard criticise someone they didn't know.

Oh, she wished her mum were with her now, and at that moment, she felt the warm gentle motion of a tear rolling down from the corner of her eye into her hair line. How could she tell her mum all this? How could she tell her mum everything that had happened? Not only was she letting her boys down, she was letting her mum down, her nieces, all the people who believed in her, and most of all she was letting herself down.

Her breathing became shallow and laboured and the paramedics were talking about what was happening… "milligrams of this, heart rate dropping, breathing erratic… need to get there quick…" all of it sounding as though she was back underwater where she belonged.

She imagined herself floating, sun on her face, bobbing along on the crest of the waves miles out to sea. The silence of it all, just the gentle rise and fall of the waves. She took a deep breath in, and her heart stabilised, breathing returned to normal and her eyes in the REM stage of wherever she was.

She knew where she was, she was at sea, with the dolphins, just her and the wide-open ocean, no one else around and she felt safe, so very safe and she knew in that moment that there was no way she wanted to be on land. It wasn't her place, land wasn't safe. On land people hurt each other, on land people abused each other, on land nothing made sense, but here, out on the ocean, floating along, this is where everything made sense.

When she came round she was in the hospital. She didn't know how she got there, but she was on a bed with the catheter in her arm and asking for a cup of tea. She was grabbing her chest and wincing in pain every time she breathed. Apparently, she had been 'a tad lucid love' as one of the nurses spoke with her in a broad Sheffield accent.

"Did you think of anyone to call to be here with you? The paramedics have called the pizza place and they are looking after your son until his friend and his mum get there. Is your partner coming to be with you?"

Pizza place? How did they know about the pizza place? She had her phone in her hand. Thinking about who to call. There was no-one in her phone she could call to come and be with her. They were either all at home with their own families or at work. So much for community.

She noticed she'd sent Joe a message letting her know where she was. She didn't remember sending it, but there it was as plain as day staring back at her.

His response: *Lots of traffic this end of town at the moment. In the pub with the boys.*

Her response to him was to tell him not to bother, she'd be home before they knew. Enjoy your drink and say hi to the boys. Now she remembered. The boys and the booze came first again.

"No, I told him not to bother, too much traffic, and by the time he gets here, I'll be home anyway, right?" Moana replied.

"Well we don't know yet love, probably best someone does come and be with you. We don't know what the test results are going to show yet," the nurse pushed back.

"I'm good, thank you anyway. I'll be okay."

"That's what you modern women all say until you've collapsed on your own with nobody. No shame in having someone with you," said the nurse sternly with her left eyebrow raised and her head slightly tilted.

Moana said nothing. She was just glad to be by herself to be honest. Putting on a brave face is what she needed to stop herself from falling apart. She just had to get through these next few days. Just keep pushing through, and she would be alright. She would either be alone in a prison cell up in Scotland with no jobs to do so she could properly rest, or on holiday with her boys. Neither felt too bad right now, but one was most definitely the preferred choice.

Hearing the words 'blood clots in your heart, and possibly your lungs' had blurred into the words 'just running tests' and 'any stress of late?' Everything was in slow motion, it hurt her to breathe. She was wheeled off to some kind of x-ray room. Doctors came and went, as did the naps. She would wake up in her own bed in a moment and this would have all been a bad dream.

A few hours later the test results had come back, and they couldn't find anything physically wrong with her.

"Probably just the stress you've been under, or a reaction to the medication" she had been taking was the diagnosis. Lovely people these doctors, but did they really have any idea about what goes on in the body and why it works the way it does.

She smiled and said thank you.

"Did you want another cup of tea love?" asked one of the nurses, looking at her with such sorrow in her eyes.

Another doctor came by as she was finishing her cup of tea and told her she could return home, and the hospital would call her a taxi.

Leaving the hospital she turned to her left, and saw the wing where she had been less than a month before. Dropping her head and pushing her hands deeper into her pockets, she walked to the taxi. Climbing into the taxi she was looking forward to just having a cuddle with her boys and her dogs, drinking a cup of tea, and then going to bed.

But that wasn't going to happen, another drama was unfolding and this time she would have to be the peacekeeper.

TWELVE

THE FINAL STRAW

The last thing she expected to see as she walked into her kitchen was the paramedics and the police. The dogs were excited to see her as always and her eldest came into the kitchen to give her a big hug.

"What on earth's happening here?" she asked him.

The police were taking Joe out of the apartment in handcuffs, and the paramedics seeing to Abdu. The look of anger on Joe's face, he was saying things she couldn't actually work out due to his slurred speech. She looked at the wall in the hallway to see a bloody fist print and a couple of dents left behind. Confusion swept over her, dizziness and the loss of breath returned. What was happening to her life? To her family? What had just gone on in her home which had been such a place of warmth and love, and now here were the police, paramedics and bloody fist marks on the wall.

"Joe came back really drunk and started annoying Nabil whilst we were watching a film, so we told him to stop. He didn't like it and then started having a go at us.

Baaba told him to leave so we could watch the movie and then Joe attacked Baaba. He was really punching him, Mum. He went crazy and totally lost it. I had to pull him off Baaba and he almost turned around to hit me too."

This was all her fault, and she knew it. What had she brought into the lives of her family? Who was this person? What had happened to the kind, generous and fun-loving guy she had met back in 2015?

"Yeah you can stand there in shock, but this is all your fault! You brought him into our lives, and you stayed with a total fucking arsehole because you don't love yourself enough to know what a toxic piece of shit he is!" Abdu was up in her face now, screaming at her. Blood all over his face, his forehead battered, with a lump the size of her fist already on the right-hand side of his forehead. His face swollen and puffy, she had never seen him so messed up and angry.

She stood there in silence, there was nothing she could say other than he was right. This was her fault. She had gone back to him. But why had he come back that night when he knew she was at the hospital? Why had he gone into the house uninvited knowing Abdu would be home with the boys? Didn't he realised his presence wouldn't be wanted? And to go in drunk and start teasing her youngest when he was trying to watch a movie with his older brother and his dad? Why did he do this? What the fuck was he playing at?

"Go in the room Mama and I'll make you a cup of tea," said he eldest. "There are two more police officers in there who want to speak with you, find out what's going on."

She made her way into the lounge, feeling like she was gliding. None of this was happening. It had to be one of those nightmares she was so used to waking up to now.

"Hi, you must be Moana, I am PC Briggs and this is WPC Watts," said the male officer as he reached out his hand. "We're just wanting to ask you a few questions if you are feeling up to it. We understand you've been at the hospital. Are you okay to answer a few questions for us?"

"I'm okay thank you, but I wasn't here, so I don't know how I can help," Moana replied.

"We believe Mr Denver is your partner, and has been for a number of years?" stated WPC Watts. "We also believe your ex-husband has moved in to help with a transition of you moving out of the family home, is this correct?"

"Mr Denver and I are no longer in a relationship, not quite sure what we are to be honest, and he has been staying with some mutual friends a few miles away. And yes, whilst I prepare to move out, my ex-husband has moved in so we can do a seamless transition, well that was the plan anyway."

"Okay, so Mr Denver isn't living here then?" clarified WPC Watts.

"No. I am not sure why he was here, because like you stated, I have been at the hospital and as far as I knew he was with friends drinking after work and then going back to their place. Things haven't been good between us for a while, and he moved out over a month ago. He has stayed a few nights here and there, but he now lives with our mutual friends," confirmed Moana.

"Has he expressed any kind of anger like this before?" asked PC Biggs.

"I didn't see what happened, I wasn't here," answered Moana.

"I haven't seen him like this before," said her eldest son as he handed his mum a cup of tea. "He just lost it, and yeah, he's annoying when he doesn't get what he wants or when Mum pays us more attention than him, but I haven't seen him this angry ever."

"I am just trying to understand the situation between you and your ex-husband, and your partner." said WPC Watts.

"What's to understand? I was married, we have a great relationship, I know not many couples who get divorced do, but we are not them. I am leaving the family home to have a bit of a break and to complete a work trip and my ex-husband has moved in so there is a week's overlap so he can get to know where everything is, and so the dogs get used to him being here. Plus, I was unwell just over a month ago and Abdu has been supporting me in my recovery. Joe has stayed over on a few occasions and like I said, I don't know why he chose to come here tonight knowing I was in the hospital."

"You do realise he has been taken into custody for grievous bodily harm and assault, and to sleep off the effects of the alcohol," stated WPC Watts.

"Why would I know that? I have only just returned from the hospital myself. I don't know where this is going, or where you want to take this line of questioning. What angle are you aiming for? If he assaulted my ex-husband, and my ex-husband wants to press charges, then that is up to my ex-husband to decide. My only concern will be the impact it has on my children, and to be honest, I don't see a future with Mr Denver any longer."

"I am not trying to take the questioning in any direction Ms…"

"Moana. My name is Moana, and I work with the police, and have been doing so for a number of years. I know how this works, and it isn't going to work in this case. I cannot tell you anything more than I already have."

"Thank you, Moana" said PC Biggs. "And I just want to say it is impressive the fact you and your ex-husband have worked out an amicable resolve and agreement. It would be great if more divorced parents got along. Would certainly make our jobs easier. That said, I think it would be best if Mr Denver didn't come by the property again."

"Oh, don't worry, he won't. I don't want him anywhere near my children or me from now on." And the moment she said it there was that stabbing pain in her heart again, the doubt within her mind. Who was she trying to kid? These feelings were messed up and everything that she resolved to do to be rid of this man from her life, the lives of her children, they were as much about convincing herself as they were declaring them to the police, her ex-husband, and the Universe. He had assaulted her ex-husband in a bad way, been taken to the police station on assault charges and made a hole in the brick wall of her hallway. Thank God this was an old property! If it had been a new build, his fist would have gone through the plasterboard into next door.

She couldn't have him in the house again. She couldn't allow him in her life any longer. It had to be over, all she had to do was end it. But how? She'd already ended it twice and now look where they all were.

She walked the police officers to the door, and then went to check on her youngest, who was thankfully fast asleep… and oh, so cute with it. No longer a baby, but a grown boy, almost in his teen years, and such an amazing soul.

How could she have brought him into their lives? How could she have taken him back after what had happened a few weeks ago? Stayed with him after Spain, and Italy, and the court cases? What was it that he had over her that made her keep letting him back into her life? The promises that he loved her, the small efforts he made and then let slip, giving her false hope all the time, or the face that the future picture they had created together was so in alignment with one another? It was like he was the perfect match, and he always knew when to say the right things, and the best way to make her think it was all her fault, get inside her head, and she knew it. So why did she stay?

"Mama? Are you okay?" asked her eldest son. "You look miles away. What happened at the hospital? What's wrong? Is it the migraines again?"

"I was miles away Baaba. I just can't believe all this is happening. I am so, so sorry. You deserve better than this, you and your brother, and look at what I have brought upon our family."

"It's not your fault, you weren't here. You can't control what happens. You weren't to know he was going to be here or do what he did. Is he gone for good this time?" comforted her son Kamel.

"I hope so. I really do. And I am okay, the doctor ran

some tests and they believe it is stress and anxiety of everything that is going on, what with the court cases and the move, leaving you boys and the dogs. This is a big trip in so many ways Baaba, and it isn't easy."

"But you have to do this Mama, you need a rest. You know you do, and we'll be alright. We can eat pizza every night, whilst playing computer games and getting fat," Kamel replied with a cheeky grin on his face.

"I know, and that's what worries me!" laughed Moana. "I am just so sorry, I didn't mean to worry you, or bring this much chaos to our family. Nothing like this ever happened…"

She was going to finish the sentence when Kamel jumped in and said, "Before he came on the scene. You should get rid of him Mum. He's not good for you, and it's not just about us deserving better, you deserve better."

They hugged and she cried, he told her to go to bed and that he would walk the dogs. So, as she was getting washed ready for bed, Kamel walked the dogs and she waited for him to come back in. They hugged once more and then went to bed.

In the early hours of the next morning, Abdu came back to the apartment. He'd had stitches in his head and Moana woke up to see how he was. Abdu was okay to begin with but then he started having a go at her for bringing the arsehole into their family. And as he started shouting at her the pains in her chest came back, and before she knew it she was coming round with a paramedic either side of her. Both her boys and Abdu stood there with her, Kamel angry at his dad for causing his mum to drop to the floor and stress her out and Nabil looking scared and worried in the background, holding onto the dogs.

The paramedics wanted her to go back to the hospital, but she wouldn't. She wanted to get her things ready for the trip up north for the court case. It would take her 13 hours to get to where she was going, and she needed to go over her notes and meet with her lawyer friend one last time. She promised she would take it easy.

Neither of the boys wanted to leave her and go to school, so Abdu phoned the school and explained that Moana had been in hospital and had the paramedics out and that the boys would be home from school for the day. The school authorised the absence and wished Moana a quick recovery. It was a day of sleeping and resting for everyone, and although Abdu wanted to press charges against Joe, it was agreed he wouldn't because the boys would be called as witnesses and neither Moana nor Abdu wanted to put the boys through it all. Joe had got away with his aggressive behaviour yet again, and would no doubt say he didn't remember, just like he did in Italy.

The day to travel up north for the court case came, and Moana was nervous. She still had the tightness of breath and felt dizzy, but she had to go. She told her lawyer once she had got there what had happened and the Judge was advised.

The day passed with a successful result and Moana went to her favourite restaurant in the town. It was almost a steppingstone to say goodbye as this was where her and Joe had had their first date.

After dinner she headed back to her AirBnB to relax and sleep. She fell into a deep sleep and woke up with just an hour to spare before her train went back down south. It wasn't her favourite birthday, but it was a celebration of sorts. This was the beginning of the end and this was the start of a new journey.

Back in Sheffield, she had just two days before her birthday celebrations went ahead in her favourite local Italian restaurant. Friends came from all over the country and Joe was there too. He was ignored by a handful of them and they couldn't understand what he was doing there. Confused looks crossed the table and when she had a moment, she admitted she was scared to tell him not to be there.

He made jokes about his hand being all bandaged up and the pins he was going to need in his hand, but no-one was buying it. A few eyebrows were raised, especially by Kamel who by this time had had all he could take of Joe.

There was a discrepancy at the end of the night with the bill, a shortfall of about £200. As always there was Joe in front of everyone, telling them not to worry, he would cover it. Funny how he always had the money in front of others, but never any money when it came to paying hotel bills, mobile phone bills or contributing to food in the apartment.

She let this one slide and accepted gracefully. She only had a few more days in his company and then she was gone with her boys on a holiday of a lifetime. Thanks, and gratitude was shared, goodbyes were said along with best wishes and then those who were headed back up the hill to the apartment, gathered their coats and walked the ten minutes together in good spirits.

A few more friends stopped by to wish Moana happy

birthday and the best of luck on her journey. Abdu had chosen to sit this one out and gone to a friend's house for the night. With a bottle of champagne and two bottles of prosecco gifted to her for her birthday – plus a bottle of amaretto, her favourite for making Tiramisu – she thought about what to do with it all. She was ready to go to bed, and as everyone but Joe and her friend Lisa were the only ones who remained, she said her goodnights and went to bed.

She woke up the next morning to find Joe in bed beside her, and as she went through to the lounge she saw her friend Lisa on the couch. Why had Joe not slept on the couch and Lisa in the guest room? She was confused, and why the fuck was he in her bed? Looking over at her dining room table she noticed all the bottles of alcohol empty. The champagne, the prosecco, and the amaretto. WTAF? Surely the pair of them could not have drank all the bottles by themselves? And why would they? They were not theirs to drink. They had been hers, her birthday and celebration gifts, not a bloody free for all! How dare they!

Lisa came through to the kitchen as Moana was making coffee.

"Morning Moana," said Lisa sounding fragile.

"Not impressed Lisa, not impressed," responded Moana, with a followup question of what time was her train and pretty much a demand of when to leave, like as soon as possible.

The excuses and the apologies came and then Joe came through into the kitchen, looking annoyed at having been woken up and offended at having been accused of drinking all 'her drink' when it had been left on the table for guests.

Moana's blood was boiling, and she was ready to explode, and then the pain in her chest came back as if to remind her that she only had one more day to get through and then it would all be over. Joe disappeared into the bathroom for ages for a bath, without asking anyone if they needed the loo or wanted to have a wash themselves. Moana's boys woke up to the sounds of the voices, and the bath running.

"I need the toilet Joe," said Kamel as he knocked on the bathroom door.

"For fuck's sake, can't a man get a bath in his own home anymore?" snapped Joe as he came out of the bathroom with just a towel around his waist.

"It's not your home, and I don't know why you're even here. No one wants you here," said Kamel as he entered the bathroom.

Moana couldn't help being proud of her son for standing up and speaking out at Joe, but worried that Joe would turn on Kamel as he came back out of the bathroom. But Joe said nothing, just stood and glared at Moana. She said nothing and yet the silence said everything.

The day passed without incident and Joe was quietly watching his programmes on his laptop on the couch ignoring everyone whilst Moana and the boys got their things together for the holiday. Joe then left and went to see their friends up the road and sort out a surprise night in their AirBnB which he had arranged for him and Moana, a last night together.

She had wanted to spend it at home with her dogs, but what could she say? Did she really want to cause a scene on the last night and risk another trip to the hospital or more violence from him? So, she went along with it. Sleeping next to each other, he didn't even hug her. Here she was alone with him, an opportunity to be intimate and nothing. Not even a cuddle or a kiss goodnight. She regretted going and wished she had stayed at home with her boys, her dogs and her ex-husband.

The next day she headed back to her apartment to say her goodbyes and thanks to Abdu, say goodbye to her dogs, which made her sob her heart out. When would she see them again? Her heart was breaking in so many different ways, and then Abdu came and gave her a hug and told her to enjoy herself, to rest, to heal and to not worry. Everything would be fine. This would be a great opportunity for him and the boys to get to know each other again and for them all to step up together.

This was a time for her, and she needed this time. If anything, the trip to the hospital had proven that. They embraced each other again and smiled at each other. The love she felt for him was still buried deeply within her, and although she was no longer in love with him, she still loved him dearly and was so grateful for the love and support, the caring and the encouragement he gave her. He was the only one who knew just what this trip was truly about. He knew the trauma she was about heal from and she knew the depths of her soul she would have to go to, and knowing her, would go to so she could become the mum she always wanted to be.

She had to let go of all the blame she had piled on herself, all the shame she felt about being a bad mother, the embarrassment at not being able to let go of this guy who had almost destroyed her, and guilt she felt about leaving their boys and her dogs. The belief that she had let her boys down weighed heavily on her, but the belief that she was not a good mother or the mother she wanted to be, the mother they needed her to be was going to be her biggest hurdle.

This time was for her to stop pushing down all the guilt, stop pretending that everything was okay, stop putting on a brave face and doing things for others. This was her time, her time to heal herself, and discover who she truly was. To start believing in herself again, to become the one who everyone believed in and the woman who would eventually change the world.

Abdu reminded her of all of this in one single look, and one single sentence of, "You've got this. Go do you, and just remember, this will always be your home."

But she knew it could never be her home again. There were too many memories there. Too much trauma and too many nights where she had cried herself to sleep, too many days when she had slid down the wall in deep despair crying and wailing in deep pain. There was no way the apartment could ever be her home again. Maybe she would visit again, but she could never live there again. This was goodbye, goodbye to a life she had wanted to build with her boys, and it had all been wiped out by the unfortunate meeting of a man named Joe.

THIRTEEN

THE LEAP OF FAITH

Time with her boys, far away from the UK, away from the day-to-day responsibilities, the reminders of everything that had happened was just what she needed. What they all needed. They had been through a lot over the past ten years. Civil war, relocation and re-integration from one culture to another, divorce, death, bullying, arrests, foster care, court cases and the rebuilding of lives in two new homes and three new schools. It was a lot to process, a lot to cope with and grow from.

The first week all they wanted to do was sleep, they had a lot of travelling to do to get to their first destination and there they would be locked away in a magical land of nature and healing. They would be taken care of, loved on, given space to just be, nourish their bodies with clean organic foods, as well as enjoy swimming in the streams and ocean, surfing, hiking in nature.

As the weeks passed by, they travelled to so many different locations in this new land, met with friends old and new, ate out at some fab places, took part in some adrenalin activities and just had the fun they had been needed for a long time. They bonded on a deeper level and learnt more about each other. Celebrated birthdays both on land and on the water, visited museums and tropical botanical gardens, and as the weeks were coming to an end, Moana's heart started to crack open. She was going to miss spending time with her boys. She was going to miss their laughter, their scents, their bickering, their peaceful and serene faces as they slept, and most of all she was going to miss being in their energy.

She needed to heal though, and she couldn't do this and be the mother she wanted to be whilst back in the UK. She couldn't lead her children by example, or to greatness if she stayed. She couldn't be the mother they deserved and needed by staying in the UK. She had to go, and she had to purge the trauma from her body, cleansing herself of the evil that had happened, and the nasty energies which had attached themselves to her. Most of all, she needed to sleep.

For five weeks she didn't respond to anyone back in the UK, this was her time with her boys. Their time with their mama. This was about them and no one else. No one else outside of them mattered. She didn't know when she would see them again, or where, all she knew was that they needed a mother who wasn't broken, or broke, or dropping to the floor, not sleeping at night. They needed a mother who was firing on all cylinders and not on her way to an early grave.

The final day came when she had to say goodbye. Watching them head off confidently to their departure gate so they could fly back by themselves halfway around the world was a huge moment in all their lives. The boys were now entering a different stage in their own personal responsibility, stepping up to a new level of maturity, and knowing their parents were confident in their ability to do so, whilst trusting them to behave and take care of each other, was a huge confidence boost for them both. Moana watched, proudly as they walked confidently through the security gates, tears falling with a mixture of loss, grief, relief, and exhaustion.

She felt a void appear in the centre of her body and a loss of breath that no amount of words could describe. This was make or break time. This was an opportunity to heal, to grow and to make a difference in the world, one in which her boys would become men, and it all started with herself. She was no good to anyone else right now, and she couldn't serve and take care of others if she wasn't serving or taking care of herself. She had a place to stay, and a plan of action but first she needed to sleep.

She checked in with Abdu and her mum, let them know the boys were on their way back and she was now about to take the biggest leap of faith she had ever taken, not just in herself, but in her boys and Abdu too: stepping back so they could all step up into the men they were born to be.

Speaking with her mum the tears fell and it seemed they would never stop. Her children had been gone for more than 24 hours, and yet the thought of not seeing them in the weeks and months to come was tearing her apart.

Her mum didn't know the true depth of why she was doing this, she had her own ideas, but the understanding she had was that her daughter needed time to heal from the court case, the relationship breakdown and the shock of becoming a single mum after being married for 15 years. She didn't know about the rape, or the gang rape. She didn't know about the night Joe had turned on her daughter in Italy. All she knew was her daughter needed time to focus on herself, to regain her strength, confidence, and focus. Her daughter was strong, but just like granite when it is chipped away at for long enough, it still cracks and breaks. She had hated seeing what her daughter had been through, but she also knew this time away would be the best thing in the long run for everyone concerned. She was proud of her daughter, for taking a stand for herself and other women, to go after her dream, but to also acknowledge that she needed to do this for herself. To coach and lead other women to greatness, she needed to lead herself there first, and this trip was exactly what she needed.

"Have you spoken with him yet?" her mum asked.

"No. I don't want to. I just want to sleep and get my head around everything," Moana replied.

"You're not going to get your head around everything mate. You just need to focus on one day at a time, take your time and go with the flow."

"I miss them already, and the dogs. I miss them jumping on the bed and walking them, their cute little faces looking up at me whilst I am working," cried Moana.

"Who – the dogs or the boys?" joked her mum.

"The dogs," Moana giggled back.

"Look, you've made this choice. And if in six months you feel better, and you realise this is not what you want, then you can always come back home." her mum reassured her.

"I know. I have to go now. I'll call you over the next few days once I have slept okay. Tell Dad I love him, love you too."

"Love you too, and remember, if anyone can make this work, you can. And you're not just doing this for yourself remember. You're doing this for those boys of yours, and women the world over. Women like me who never got the opportunity as well as young girls like your nieces. You go and do this, and you give it your bloody best shot. Alright?"

"Yes Mum. I love you. Night, night."

"Night, night. And be careful!" and with that Moana switched off her phone and headed to the place she was staying for the next few nights. She needed sleep; tomorrow was the start in a new phase of her life. A new chapter for her, her boys, and women the world over.

The next morning, she woke up to the alarm to say the boys should be landing at any moment. She didn't like to switch her phone on first thing in the morning or check her phone for messages or Facebook updates as soon as she woke up. She much preferred to focus more on her journaling and creative process.

Checking the flight checker, it looked like their flight was on time. She let out a breath and got on with her journaling, checking her phone every five minutes to see if the boys had made it through immigration, passport control, security, even though she knew they would be anything up to an hour getting through.

She checked in with Abdu and he was there to meet

them and gave her updates from down on the ground at his end.

Although she saw multiple messages from Joe, asking how things were going, emojis of love and kisses, she ignored them. It was confusing her all over again, especially as he had been searching for opportunities for her and 'hoping it was going well'. How could she continue with him after everything? But how could she not when he was being so lovely, so supportive and loving? Had the distance made the heart grow fonder for him already? His messages were like they were at the beginning, before all the crazy shit started, was it really a case of they were starting over again?

Receiving a message from Abdu with the boys arrival back in the UK, she suddenly relaxed. Her shoulders dropped and she lay back on her bed offering gratitude up to the heavens above. "Thank you God for delivering my boys back home safely. Please take care of them." Warm tears rolled down her face with mixed emotions passing through her.

The next thing she knew she was waking up and it was dark. What time was it? How long had she been asleep? She sat up, looked at the clock on her wall and had a drink of water. Tomorrow, or rather later that day she was heading out to get this trip underway, so she had better get back to sleep so she was ready.

She was back to sleep before she knew it and woke up with a new level of energy. There had been no nightmares, no waking up with hot sweats, just a deep and peaceful sleep. The first deep sleep she'd had in a long time. Grabbing her bag and a map of the country, it was time to explore what was truly possible, for herself. Could she make this work? Could this time by herself, learning about herself, be the answer she needed to break the cycle of the last three years?

Travelling around the country, discovering new places, dealing with a different culture was great to begin with, but she soon found out that the way she was living was not going to be sustainable. She was choosing locations with private rooms, or entire places to herself. It just wasn't safe being in a place with other people. What if they spiked her? What if the woman went out and the man was left alone if she stayed in an AirBnB? What if the location wasn't safe when she got there? What if this, what if that, what if everything. Over analysing the safety aspects of everything, almost to the point of paralysing paranoia, the anxiety was coming back. Her chest tightening and the dizziness of even just being in a public place. On the outside when in public she was friendly, in public she could suck it up and get on with it all, she could put on the mask of everything being okay, appear brave to the world, but inside she felt like the biggest fraud there was.

If she continued to suck it up and push the fear and anxiety down, then she would not get to the point of healing she needed to do. Hiding away in her room when staying in AirBnBs wasn't the answer either. She needed to meet people, be confident meeting people, stop hiding behind the shyness, and stop hiding behind the badass woman who had it all together.

As the weeks went by, her confidence slowly grew. She would head down to the marina to meet people, network with the marina office managers, apply for jobs on boats and sit in the cafés writing. If she was going to get to know the locals, she had to start meeting them, putting herself out there, telling people what she was doing.

The fear of being alone in an office with a guy, especially if he offered her a coffee, cup of tea or glass of water sent her internals into panic.

What if he put something in her drink?

But why would he do that?

What if they introduce her to a dodgy boat owner?

Why would they do that?

What if, but why, what if, but why… back and forth, back and forth the dialogue went until she realised her own ridiculousness.

Her fear may have started from a scary place, but the likelihood of anything happening to her in the places she was visiting, in broad daylight, and the kind of people she was asking, there was a very small risk involved in staying or working in certain locations, or traveling with certain people.

Choosing to stay in hostels was a whole new experience, something she had never done before, but it introduced her to people, helped her learn about other places, she picked up travel tips and learnt which areas and hostels to stay away from. She loved the community vibe of the kitchens, and soon realised how to choose them so she didn't end up in grotty places with the millennials who were just interested in partying and drinking.

Being in completely different time zones to her boys was one of the hardest aspects, as she was not able to speak with them as often as she would have liked. Giving Abdu the space to be a parent without her being around was proving harder than she expected, and harder than he expected too.

He admitted he had underestimated the role of a single parent because she had made it look so easy, as if she had a team of people around her. Hearing this from Abdu made her cry. She felt seen, heard, and acknowledged. She had to withhold telling him how she ran things and had to allow him the opportunity to figure things out by himself as she had done over the years.

He would ask her how she was feeling being by herself, and how she was sleeping, if the anxiety was subsiding and a whole host of other thoughtful gestures. He asked for her advice and gave her some from all of his travels alone over the years. He encouraged the boys to respond to her messages, making sure they realised that they were also responsible for keeping the relationship between them alive.

Joe had been calling and messaging, and due to the loneliness and the kind of messages he had been sending, she ended up on the phone with him for almost an hour every day. It felt safer somehow to know she was in a relationship – no matter how dysfunctional and unhealthy it was, something she had started to acknowledge.

Being alone and eating out by herself, whether it was a salad on the beach or a meal in a restaurant, she would notice how couples of all ages would be interacting, and pick up on the energy between them. She realised there was so much she had not seen in relationships, so much which had been lacking in both her marriage and her relationship with Joe.

Lying alone at night crying due to the depths of

loneliness and the messed-up stuff that had happened, had finally started to subside. The joy of having a large bed all to herself was proving to be a great thing too, and it was always made as soon as she got out of it.

Eating what she wanted, when she wanted it, also great. Going where she wanted without checking in with anyone or having to compromise was also proving to be a fun thing to do. Reading, exploring, going to museums, working as many hours as she liked, not having to think about anyone else for the first time in her life was strange and exciting all at the same time.

Sometimes she would get so excited she would giggle to herself as she walked down the street. Dancing and singing wherever she went, it wasn't long before she realised she was happier than she had been in a long time. She had found out about so many opportunities that her mission to travel around the world was looking like it might actually become a thing, rather than just an idea, or a possibility. She was meeting people who were introducing her to other people, and more opportunities were coming her way, she didn't really have time to think about being lonely or afraid.

Until she sailed up north for a regatta. She knew this was a great opportunity, she knew this was going to push her out of her comfort zone, and she knew she would be surrounded by alcohol, men drinking, and she had to be okay with it. The mistress of sucking it up and putting on a brave face, knowing she knew how to be friendly, and how to pull a good pint from having worked in pubs and hotels in her late teens, she would be okay. Focusing her mind on the fact that 'This was business. This was sailing' was the comfort blanket she needed. There was nothing to be afraid of and she knew she trusted herself more. She had started to tell herself she didn't drink either, and working behind the bar in front of everyone allowed her to observe behaviours, and meet as many of the sailors racing as possible. She was safe behind the bar, and she would be there to clear up long after everyone else had gone back to their boats or their hotels. She could do this. No pretending to be brave. She was brave. She could choose it over and over again throughout the night.

Over the week she had got to know quite a few sailors, and a good many contacts who were encouraging her on her journey. She was invited to do a boat delivery back to the capital city along the coast. It would take a few days, and there would be two other crew members. Both men. Part of her wanted to run and hide, the other part of her wanted to jump for joy that she had been invited to do her first boat delivery. She was incredibly nervous, and thoughts of what had happened before she'd left the UK just kept going over and over in her mind.

She offered to go meet the captain the next day and discuss the opportunity. Before she gave herself time to back out and step into fear, she accepted; and then lay awake all night worrying about what would happen. How could she protect herself? How could she keep herself safe? How could she make sure neither of them tried anything? Playing scenario after scenario over in her head brought back all the memories of the pain, the upset and the fear. This was not a healthy space to be in, and that's when she was reminded of what Joe would say to her after he would reel her in and then ignore her. "Don't put your head there, you don't need to go there, it's not a healthy space to be in."

Everything was reminding her of him, of how he had helped her learn to breathe, the foods she loved, the songs she sang, the ideas for her future business, identical replicas to the ones he said he wanted. No wonder it had been easy to fool her into loving him, and then when he had her in close, he would disappear, not speak with her for days, see her messages, and her replies to his comments on Facebook and then ghost her – both publicly and privately – before telling her that it was only her he spoke with on the phone; something she believed until she spoke with mutual friends and found out by pure chance that they had been speaking just a few days earlier.

He was messing with her head, with her emotions, and she needed time away from him and social media. An opportunity he had sent her had proven to be very successful and would help her immensely. Part of her didn't want to take it because he had set it up, she didn't want him to use it against her in the future, but it was an opportunity that was just too great to turn down. She got along with the family and she felt safe in the company of the older man who was the captain and owner of the yacht.

There were so many great things about Joe it was hard not to love him, and he had his challenges like everyone, baggage like everyone, and now they were tens of thousands of miles apart, she was safe. No harm had come to her at all. Something that had been weighing on her mind.

But when he called when he said he would, and sent

her loving messages it was hard to not respond. Surely you couldn't fake love like this, and keep up the act? Had he realised how amazing she was, and so was now making the effort to be in touch more, wanting to make amends for everything that had gone before? Was this his way of proving that he was really the guy for her? That he could keep his promise of keeping up with her, regardless of how fast she evolved.

And there was that reminder of the fact that they had not been physically intimate for 18 months, and the last time she'd had sex was when those guys had pinned her down and raped her. He couldn't even bring himself to make love to her before she left, knowing she knew the last time she had had a man inside of her, it had been against her will. What kind of partner did that?

She had one more trip to make before leaving on the yacht with the gentleman who she would be sailing all the way to the Caribbean with, so she headed south and arrived at the location where she would be spending three weeks working on a boat taking people out to see dolphins, seal colonies and albatross.

She would also be staying in a mixed dorm in a hostel, something she had never done before and something that worried her. She made sure she slept in leggings and a t-shirt and slept in the top bunk, something she had not done since she shared a room with her sister when they were both teenagers.

It was an interesting experience, not one she ever wanted to repeat but she used it as a victory on her way to coming to terms with being in close proximity to men again. Two guys shared the dorm with her, and two other women – and it was in the staff quarters so safer than simply sharing a dorm with hostel guests.

One of the guests who arrived made her laugh, they hit it off, were both divorced and had businesses. They had a lot to talk about, and so went out to dinner together. They had a great night, and it was the first time she had been alone with a guy in public for something other than business or sailing.

Later that night he asked to sleep with her. She was not someone who slept with men she hardly knew. She'd been in an 18-year relationship with her ex-husband, married for 15 of those years. She had then been in a relationship with Joe for three years. When it came to dating or sleeping with men, she was actually a novice, and really quite shy. The thought of sleeping with someone by choice rather than continuing to know that the last time she'd had sex had been by force made her think the offer over. He was an attractive guy, funny, and she liked him. Could she do this? Would this mean she was cheating on Joe? Did it even really matter considering everything she had been through?

He had chosen to become celibate over a year earlier and left her celibate by default. She was a woman who wanted to heal, so she said yes, she would have sex with him. If she died whilst at sea, at least she wouldn't die having the gang rape as her last experience of sex.

She was nervous, scared even. Would she feel anything? Would it hurt her? Was she disfigured down there? Would the damage, if it was still visible, be noticeable and would it repulse him? She didn't know the answer to any of these questions and wouldn't know until she experienced it again. He led her by the hand to his room and could tell she was scared. He told her not to worry, not to be afraid and if at any time she wanted to stop just to let him know. It was like he was reading her mind and continued to do so in one of the most beautiful sexual experiences she'd had.

Afterwards she went back to her room, and instead of feeling dirty, instead of feeling ashamed, instead of feeling guilty, she felt relieved. He hadn't noticed anything, and if he had, he didn't say anything. He had been a complete gentleman all night, and for that she was truly grateful. She was proud of herself for having had the courage to allow herself to be with another man, and the beauty of it was after he left the next day, she would never have to see him again.

The next day her fellow crew members noticed she was quieter, she was calmer, and back at the hostel, the manager had started to be spiteful towards her. Where she had been friendly, the woman was now just plain rude. Then she came out with her jealous rampage, throwing the night before in her face. "How do you think Joe would feel knowing you had cheated on him? Think you're so fucking perfect sat out here every night working on your business or studying and talking to your kids. What do you think they would think of their mother if they knew you slept with random guys all the time?"

Moana didn't answer, just let the woman vent. She knew nothing about the situation, and she knew nothing about what it had just taken for her to do what she had done. No one would make her feel guilty for what had happened. One thing Moana did now know though was that she no longer wanted to be with Joe. How could she now she had been with another man, regardless of the reasons behind it? Now she just had to tell him, and stick to it this time.

With preparations made to cross the Pacific Ocean, her mum and her boys having the contact details of the boat, date of expected arrival and the owner's family's phone numbers, she felt safe and looked after. She had taken to calling the owner Uncle and had enjoyed the weeks leading up to the first leg of the trip where they would meet additional crew members.

Joe had called her and was his now regular lovely self. She was too excited about the trip to remember to tell Joe what had happened, and so they had yet another lovely call together. She knew she loved him still, but she also knew deep in her soul he was no good for her. Being away at sea would give her time to think, time to figure everything out. Isn't that what everyone says anyway, that people run away to sea to either figure things out or hide from their problems?

Moana often wondered to herself if she was running away from her problems, but considering this trip had been planned for a long time before the 13th October 2017 – a date that was still etched in her mind – just brought forward by a few years earlier, was all the proof she needed to tell herself that she wasn't running away. Did she need to give herself any proof? She didn't want to think so, but she still kept searching for it.

She had been accused by many people that she was being selfish; told by mothers that she was being neglectful of her children because she wasn't at home taking care of them (and their every whim). Men told her that she was damaging future relationships and creating separation anxiety, abandonment, and rejection issues within her boys, not to mention that she thought more of her social media presence and public profile than she did her own children. Some of these comments coming from people she loved, had been friends with for years, and people she chose to walk away from, because if they really thought that, then they didn't know her in the first place.

She'd been away from home on this trip now for what was almost five months and she had been going over and over in her mind that the day she left to cross the ocean, she would miss her flight back to the UK. She was having to choose herself all over again.

She had a call arranged with her children in the morning, which would be late evening in the UK, so she would discuss it with them then. She so wanted to go, but if she went, then she would miss her flight. She had already sorted out things with the tax office in the UK, told them her plans, arranged for letters to be sent from the boat owner to confirm the role and payment she would be getting. Everything was set, all she had to do was choose herself, and the bigger plan she and her boys had come up with.

During the call she told the boys what the situation would be. Their eyes rolled so loudly they could have woken the dead. "Really? Are we even having this conversation? You HAVE to do this! This is good for you. You need this, and anyway we are getting fat on pizza and watching movies until really late into the night and early mornings, having wild parties and playing computer games all day and not going to school." This made her laugh. She had the best boys ever, and their understanding of the situation may have larger pieces of the puzzle missing, but they understood the bigger picture and that was the best part about it.

Joe called her the morning she was due to set sail, and the way he looked at her melted her heart. She couldn't help but smile and feel excited to be speaking with him. He had set this opportunity up and now she was getting to deepen her knowledge of sailing and cross an ocean, away from land for days, with no land in sight for at least seven of them. Her childhood dream was coming true. She was doing this!

The ocean crossing was fraught due to the couple who had joined her and the Uncle. The sailing was amazing, but the company was just not her cup of tea. Even the Uncle had changed his attitude and was a very different man in the company of the married couple who joined. Everyone else was seasick and so Moana being Moana put down the attitude problems to the fact that everyone else was seasick. She tried not to be so happy and joyful all the time, but she was far away from land, watching dolphins play and alone at night under the stars, on a boat and in silence. It was blissful, and just what she needed.

At the six-month marker, the day her flight was booked to return to the UK, they were anchored off a remote island with crystal clear waters in the middle of the Pacific Ocean. The others all wanted to go to the resort for the day and couldn't understand why she would want to stay on the boat by herself. It was a really emotional day, not just because here she was in paradise, on a boat all to herself, getting a taste of the life she had always wanted and loving it, but it was a measuring point of how far she had come in such a small amount of time.

She had learnt a lot about herself, a lot she liked, and the bits about herself she didn't like, she had gotten to focus on and improve. More than that though, she had become comfortable in her own skin. She had started to trust her instincts, trust that she was a nice person, even if others didn't think so. She knew that her life was heading in the direction she wanted it to, and most of all she knew her boys were proud of her.

So, on the day she was supposed to fly back to the UK – a place which she was unsure would ever be her home again – she sat by herself and allowed the tears to fall. The pain of the guilt she felt for leaving her boys, the shame and dirtiness from the rapes fall away because neither of them were her fault. No means no, and even though she still had no memories of the nights she was spiked and raped in both Spain and Sheffield, she was able to come to terms with what had happened and release it.

After hours of journaling, crying, and praying, she decided to go snorkelling. Getting in the ocean, baptising herself with the sea salt water, watching the fish and almost choking herself because she got too excited and forgot how to breathe in her excitement. She cleansed her soul. Turning over onto her back, she floated, allowed herself to be held by the water, held by the Universe, and meditated and gave gratitude for all that had happened *for* her, not *to* her.

Choosing this new distinction was more powerful, gave her the strength she needed to move forward, to take the lessons from all the negatives and ponder on how she could use what had happened *for* her so she could serve humanity on a whole other level. Raising great young men was one way, being a kind and caring individual was one way, but turning the negatives into positives, this was a whole other level of consciousness and service to God, to Universe, to Source, whatever people wanted to call it.

Having witnessed everything she had witnessed whilst at sea, and whilst on land, how could she deny the creation of the energy life force behind it all? She couldn't and didn't want to.

FOURTEEN
THE PATTERNS EMERGING

Invited to some of the parties, Moana didn't trust the intentions of some of the men, so kept herself on the dancefloor and away from those who made her feel uncomfortable. A big victory in itself as she had wanted to go back to the boat and get into her bunk. Instead she chose to stay.

Plucking up the courage to actually go to the parties had been the biggest win for her. She was one of a few single women, amongst married couples and single men, and – according to many of the women – she was flirting with the husbands and sleeping with the single men. That couldn't have been further from the truth.

After the time with the divorced businessman a few weeks before, she hadn't even considered being with another man, nor did she want to be. She had done what she needed to do to erase the thought of the last time – being, the gang rape – and that was all she needed right now.

The thought of being with one of the married men

horrified her and she saw the depth of insecurities these women had in their own self and their marriages. It was a reminder of how the married women had treated her when her and Abdu had got divorced. Women were just not very confident in their relationships and she didn't want to be one of those women. She wanted to be in a relationship with herself first and foremost.

She'd had enough doubting and second guessing being in a relationship with Joe. And now she was back on land again, and she had helped him get another dream job, she was of no use to him at all. Realising he had just used her again so she would help him with his CV and get a job, he'd made her feel used and dirty all over again. It had become another pattern she had spotted, and now all the friendliness and the loving messages had stopped, she started to look at other patterns that had been occurring with other people in her life.

She was the common denominator in all of it, and she had to be the one to break these patterns of behaviours and stop attracting people who used her. Where was she using herself? What destructive patterns was she stuck in? With another ocean crossing coming up, she would have plenty of time to reflect, but now it was time to restock the boat for the next adventure.

Being on a boat with three other people who were seasick the moment the boat had started moving in the water wasn't much fun, and especially not when she had noticed certain things were amiss.

Trusting her instincts, she raised some issues which she thought were either dangerous or going to cause problems. The arrogance of the other crew members being what it was meant they didn't take her seriously, so she figured out by herself what was wrong and what was needed, just in case.

Trusting her instincts was becoming her litmus test. Did it feel right? Was there any hesitation? Did she have any nagging doubts? Now that she didn't drink, her intuition was getting stronger and stronger, she was going to rely on it and trust it. She had to, especially when her suspicions were proven correct with the rigging on a couple of occasions. She was glad she had prepared; she had saved them a lot of problems; as well as hours of motoring and additional hours at sea which were not necessary.

Back on land after another two weeks at sea crossing the Pacific, Moana contacted her boys to let them know she was good, had really enjoyed the sailing, sent them some pictures and then messaged her mum too.

It was also time to have a conversation with the owner of the boat because things were not working out. It was time to part company, and she was now really going to have to trust her intuition. She had a place to stay for a few nights and during this time pulled out a map of the country and started making phone calls and planning the next part of her adventure. She knew she could do this, and she knew she would be safe, because she now trusted herself to trust herself to be safe. She now trusted herself to make the right judgement calls again, and this was a huge breakthrough for her.

After a couple of great nights' sleep, she set off on her journey, not replying to any of the messages from Joe, just her mum and her boys, and those showing an interest in her journey so far.

Whilst on Facebook she saw a status update from Joe saying he was now known as the drunken one and was proud of it. It made Moana flinch, she felt repulsed by it, and again knew this was a sign that it was well and truly over between them. She knew it was, but she wanted to have that conversation with him, not end it over a text message. She then noticed he had been telling people he wanted to have more children, again a conversation he should have been having with her not everyone on Facebook, especially as he knew for her to have children again, it would more than likely kill her, something he had known going into the relationship.

Seeing this and seeing the mutual friend he was having the conversation with was just too much. It was over; with it being well and truly over when she saw a photo of him and another woman up close and personal, a woman she had suspected over a year earlier. Her instincts had been right then, and she had ignored them. Never again. She couldn't keep ignoring her intuition. It was guiding her and the more she ignored it, the worse things got.

Had she walked away from Joe in the beginning when she knew she didn't want to be in a long-distance relationship, none of the bad things that had happened, would have happened. But then if they hadn't have happened, then she wouldn't be living the life she was living now, and learning all this about herself; what she was prepared to accept, what she no longer wished to tolerate and be a part of, and she wouldn't have her two boys proud of her like they were now.

She also wouldn't have been able to inspire the women she had, and make the contacts, and promote her business the way she had, so she went back to her journal and purged all the negative emotions and wrote out all the positives that had come from the negatives. She wrote down all she had learnt about herself, all the things she had experienced since it had all happened, and everything she was grateful for.

Building a small fire on the beach, she set fire to all the pages she had just written, alchemising the positive thoughts, dreams and aspirations into being and burning all the fears, doubts and overwhelm turning the negatives into positives. She enjoyed this fire release ceremony, and she didn't care if it didn't make sense to others, it made sense to her and it seemed to be working.

During her stay at a newly refurbished and almost empty resort, she had time to process everything she had achieved, the newfound strength and confidence she had. And when Joe showed up in her messages and she told him "we need to talk" he had told her not to put her head in places it didn't need to be. He wasn't listening, or maybe he knew what was coming, but he wasn't happy that she wanted to talk, yet again.

There were parts of her that loved him dearly, and she didn't want to hurt him, but equally she loved herself more. She didn't want to be in any kind of relationship with him anymore. He had treated her badly over the years, and yes there had been some great times, but they were very few and far between. She had fallen in love with the dream they had created together, a dream he would never be able to deliver on. Plus he wanted children, had chosen celibacy and he loved alcohol more than he loved her. How could anyone be in a relationship with someone who loved any drug more than them? There was no self-respect there, and she realised that had he been the man she wanted, and deserved, he would never have allowed any harm to come to her, or to himself. He would also never have gone to the pub with their friends the night she was in hospital, and then gone to her home and attacked her ex-husband in front of her children, resulting in the police and paramedics being called. He was deeply wounded and as the saying goes 'hurt people, hurt people' and she didn't want to be hurt anymore. She wanted to be single. She wanted to discover more about herself as the woman she was today, and she wanted be a better role model for her boys, because whoever came into her life also came into the lives of her boys, and no one else was going to mess with her boys.

She had got to the point where she had to extend her visa waiver, so attended the immigration office. Hearing all about her journey and the publicly known reason why she was doing the trip, the lady was really impressed, but deeply sad that Moana had not seen her children in nine months. Fighting back the tears, Moana explained why she hoped to see her children again, but that would be months away. That upset the lady from the immigration department and inspired her all at the same time.

It was moments like this that Moana was reminded that even though people didn't know the depth of importance to her journey, the journey back to self, the journey of healing from the sexual trauma and distancing herself from Joe, people were still inspired by what she was doing. She wondered if they would actually be inspired if they knew the depth of the trips purpose, but again, it didn't matter. She was healing herself, growing in confidence being around people, learning to trust people, especially men. She had sailed with one guy who had tried it on, and she had remembered her martial arts training. And she had sailed with three incredible guys for four weeks. She had grown so much by putting herself into situations where she had to trust herself and keep her wits about her. She had grown in so many ways by saying "No" to everything and everyone who didn't take her further towards her goals, and a "Hell YES!" to everything that took her closer to the future she always dreamed of. A new improved version, without anyone else, for the time being.

When the lady from the immigration came back with all the approved documentation, she asked Moana if she would want to see her children. Moana said, "Yes, of course, but that won't happen for a couple of months at least."

The lady then smiled and said, "If I told you I have just spoken with an organisation who sponsor women, and told them about your trip and they are really impressed with you, so much so they would like to gift you a flight home this afternoon to see your children, would you accept it?"

Moana sat there stunned. She didn't quite know what to say. She had been struggling financially due to paying back money lent to her during the court cases. And now she had chosen to take back control of her life, here she was being gifted this wonderful trip back to the UK to see her children.

"I think I would have to say yes! THANK YOU!"

Both ladies cried with happiness and Moana was told

she would be welcome to come back any time in the future and it was an honour to meet her again. Not quite sure what was going on but knowing this was a great thing that was happening, Moana looked up to the heavens above and said thank you. Moana also realised that in the moments when she just allowed herself to be supported, chose based on intuition, gratitude and joy, things went well. When she was worried or afraid, and she ignored her intuition, things didn't go well.

Her arrival back in the UK was kept quiet and she spent the first few days with her mum and dad making sure they were okay and telling them as much as she could in answer to all their questions.

She called Abdu and asked him if he was going to be home later the following day as there was a parcel being delivered. Arriving back in Sheffield, she was both excited and hit by an invisible forcefield that winded her.

Her excitement to see her boys hadn't prepared her for the memories that came flooding back to her. Doing her best to focus on the positives got her so far, and she had to accept that she was now about to face the next level of healing: memories and reminders everywhere of what had happened. Would these memories and reminders trigger memories previously locked away deep inside of her, memories her subconscious had protected her from? Would she be able to move through them and come out on the other side stronger? Or would this trip back to see her boys and her dogs, set her back to the very beginning again?

FIFTEEN
THE RETURN HOME TO SELF

She'd sent Joe a message letting him know she was back, and that she wanted to see him. She knew he knew she was back; Abdu had posted a photo of her and the boys on Facebook and tagged her in it, plus the little icon in messenger had shown that the message was seen. She'd been back in Sheffield for 48 hours and had been messaged by quite a few people, some she didn't want to see again and for that she was slightly pissed off at Abdu for sharing the photo. She also found out that Joe had been told she was back, so why had he not contacted her?

She was so done with all this bullshit from him. He hadn't seen her for nine months, had been ghosting her privately and publicly, several people thought she acting like some crazy stalker who had been dumped and trying to get his attention. People could see the games he was playing, but no one said anything. Why would they? It wasn't their head he was fucking with, and no doubt he hadn't given them reason to doubt his wonderful, generous nature which had sucked her in at the very beginning and kept her hanging all this time; doubting herself, becoming paranoid, and reeling her in to get what he wanted and then tossing her aside like a worthless piece of shit. But she had allowed it to happen, she had allowed the dishonourable, disrespectful behaviour and trained him to treat her that way.

After nine months he should be knocking on her door, nine weeks and even nine days wanting to see her, kiss her and hear all about her journey; or as one friend put it, "If you had been away from me for nine days I would be ready to jump your bones into next week!" A comment which made her blush and feel attractive. And there it was, a compliment and an insight from a man who had done the inner work and had become sovereign in himself, so he could see the sovereign in women. It wasn't about the 'jumping of bones' either, it was about the journey of exploring each other's bodies, rediscovering each other's likes and dislikes, reconnecting on a deeply intimate level after having been apart for so long. Joe hadn't taken the time to find out where she was, which boats she was on, where she was heading or anything, only taking an interest in her when he needed something.

She sent him another message telling him it was over and that she hadn't wanted to end it by message, and that she was done with his ghosting, his using ways and hoped he would be happy. It was a message filled with peace, one filled with acceptance and it was a powerful message. She told him he had not left her any other choice as he had ignored her last message about being back.

He messaged back straight away, saying he had been doing her a favour, that he had let her go so she could be her, and all the other 'I'm doing you a favour' kind of comments. She told him she was no longer interested and that she deserved better, to which he said yes, you do, and in her final messages to him she told him that if he knew she deserved better, then he had been given ample opportunities to become the man he knew she deserved. She knew now that any man that truly loved a woman would become the man that he believed she deserved, would move heaven and earth to be with his Queen, and if he didn't, then he didn't love himself or her enough.

Sending Joe that message was one of the most liberating things she had done for herself in ages, and that night she went out for dinner with her boys to celebrate. Seeing people she hadn't seen for ages couldn't believe the woman they were now looking at: she was radiant, she was stronger, she was relaxed and shining so brightly she turned every head in the 70 seater fine dining restaurant – one of the few things she had missed about the UK, the fine dining cuisine, not the head turning. The head turning was something she was getting used to, and something that, although it made her feel a little uncomfortable, she was realising it was due to her energy rather than her looks – although she was looking pretty great even if she did say so herself. Her confidence was magnetic and her smile beautiful, because it didn't exist just on her lips, it came from deep within her soul and radiated out through eyes and her very being.

She was home, not home to the UK, but home to herself.

SIXTEEN

THE UNIVERSE DELIVERS

Now she was officially single, now she had set herself free of the conversation she had so badly wanted to have with Joe – even if it had been by messenger – she felt so free! The ocean had given her a sense of freedom, courage, and strength like never before, and it was wonderful because now she was harnessing it all in every area of life. Yes, she still had a way to go, but she was moving in the right direction and that was all that truly mattered.

Growing in confidence to really speak her truth, not from a space of having to prove herself to anyone, but from a place of accepting that she was valuable in her own right, regardless of what others thought of her, whether they liked her or not, had taken on a whole new depth of understanding. She wasn't looking for, or needing, words of affirmation or compliments from others. She knew she loved herself, had grown to be in love with who she was, she knew she was the person she had been looking for all her life, and she knew she could trust herself completely to make the right choices in life.

She faced demons, she faced upset, she even saw Joe in a communal space, and – even though she acknowledged him and asked how he was – he just ignored her, and then made out it was because she was speaking with someone else. His excuses just kept coming. She wanted to smile, shake her head, she had finally seen through him. Finally released herself, no longer affected by him. Facing him in this space had been the confirmation she needed that she was really done. Or was she just trying to convince herself?

A month back with her boys and fur babies, it was time to move on again. She knew this place was no longer a place she wanted to stay in. And well, the trade winds beckoned, along with her next training course. She was off to her next destination, but first she had to let the tax office know she was off again. The sooner she was free of this system the better. It was like asking permission to live her life and have them control her. She didn't like it, nor did she want to live life like this. She was to be free like her beloved ocean: free, wild, and flowing in her own direction and power.

Arriving at her location she was instantly hit with an energy she didn't like. There was something that was just not working for her. An underlying darkness. Was it the persecution she felt from wars gone by, and oppression? Was it the low vibrational people who were grossly overweight and heavily smoking? Was it because it looked like the UK had puked up its guts and the remnants of society had arrived and set up home? Was it the racism and the ignorance she saw everywhere?

It took her all of one day to walk around this whole place. A great walk up hills, through tunnels, past lighthouses, along beaches and through botanical gardens. She even witnessed some cheeky monkeys. But regardless of the great walk, she had to leave.

Back at her hostel, she made plans and called a friend in a neighbouring country over the water. She would be leaving the next day, after she cancelled her training course. The course director was surprised as she had been so keen to do the course, but she had ignored her intuition too many times and had things go wrong so there was no way was she ignoring it now. Soul said leave, so she packed her bags and was on the next ferry out of there.

Arriving in this new land, she booked into her hotel and went for a swim in their beautiful pool. Relaxing on her bed that night, she smiled to herself. She felt so different, so much lighter, so empowered. She had chosen to honour herself and taken a new direction, one she was not planning on, but it just felt so right, and tomorrow she would be with her extended family, enjoying conversations in a whole different language and one that she spoke from deep within her soul.

Travelling via train she watched the world go by, drank in the landscape, smiled to herself, felt like she couldn't contain her excitement. She felt so different that no amount of words could explain. Words cascading into her mind, wanting to be chosen for the experience she was experiencing but not one of them could take the title by themselves, until she translated them to her other language and then she smiled, then she knew what she had found… the tranquillity of her soul and it felt good, oh so good. Hmmm, so good it was almost juicy enough for her to swim in its goodness.

Making new choices, making up her own rules, going where she wanted, when she wanted and how she wanted was just so liberating and she wanted everyone to experience this great feeling. Why would anyone who knew what this felt like not want to share it with others? That would just be selfish! She had to share this with the world. She just had to!

So with her journal open, pen in hand she got to work writing down all the ideas that started falling out of her onto the pages laid out before her. Non-stop writing, non-stop smiling, giggles bubbling up inside of her and ready to explode. Every vision she had was blissful, every vision she had was either by or on the ocean. The ocean was her home, the ocean was her guide, the ocean was her playground, the ocean was her greatest teacher and ultimate mentor because it brought her back to herself in every solitary moment, every beautiful moment watching the sun and moon rise and set, the ever-changing colours of the water, the marine life, the clouds, stars, the winds; everything was just purity of self. The ocean was the greatest leveller of humanity, the greatest wakeup call and the greatest mirror of self.

As she looked out of the window, she saw it was her stop. How could that be? She had only been on the train for about half an hour. Her trip was over two hours! "WOW!" she said to herself, that went quickly, and in that moment the folding of time and space took on a whole new meaning for her. Time was simply time and time could be utilised in so many powerful ways, and the more in flow and true to self we become the more we could collapse time.

Portals, gateways, wormholes, gridlines all cascading into her mind and the book *A Brief History of Time*, which she had read and understood so deeply on the beach one afternoon came flooding back into her memory. 'Aha!' moment after 'Aha!' moment swept around her, so many things collapsing in on each other, connecting the dots like the RNA and DNA double helix which flowed within us, making each one of us so beautifully unique in this human form, but so very different depending on where our souls came from.

"Time and space, time and space, time and space," she whispered to herself as she floated off the train and into the path of her beautiful friend. The joy and love which flowed between them after almost a decade apart, the tears of joy, the non-stop chatter, the laughter, the hugs, the sisterhood, the bond of friendship which would last a lifetime. So many differences and yet so many similarities. So much to catch up on but so much more to remain unsaid because it was said in an instant with a look, a smile, a wink, and a holding of the hand.

Ten magical days with her Magribi family was just what Moana needed. She was overcome with love, with gratitude and she knew that God was so great, so, so great, and she was indeed of Divine energy herself.

Connecting to one of her online communities towards the end of her trip when she was making her choices on where to go, she noticed a meet-up across the water. She laughed. Was this really how this magic and universal alignment worked? Like, really! A woman she had wanted to meet, an author of a book she had wanted to read and a place she wanted to visit, all aligned and was only an hour across the water. And this woman was hosting an event!

She told her friend and the next thing she knew the train was booked along with the ferry ticket. The one big difference was instead of being on the first train out of there in the morning, she chose to just be in flow. She chose to take things easy and not rush, and thankfully this saved her life. Had she made the choice of the woman she was just a few months before, she would have been on the first train of the day. The seat reserved for her in first class on the first train, ended up in one of the most fatal train crashes in the country's history.

At first her and her fellow passengers had no idea about the cause of the delays, they were all just sitting around getting to know one another, taking everything in their stride. It was only when they disembarked did they find out the cause of the delay. Calling her friend to explain the situation, her friend already knew and had already arranged for her to be collected by a family friend in that area and a room for the night was waiting for her. She couldn't help but smile. Eyes towards heaven, Moana whispered, "Thank you!"

She liked this new sense of trusting the process, of trusting in herself to make the right choices, of trusting her intuition and of trusting everything was working out as it was supposed to for her highest greatness.

The next day she was taken to the train station and her new ticket was issued against the first one with ease and a smile. An hour on the ocean and then a few hours before the meet-up happened. Walking up the road out of the ferry terminal she was met with a sign that almost floored her. A sign for Cadiz, the place where she had been with Joe when he had left her unconscious and gone clubbing, resulting in the old man raping her. She was stunned. She was not prepared for this moment.

Feeling unstable, smelling the smell of the old man's breath again, hearing his voice for the first time and seeing his face in patches as it came to the fore of her mind, she needed to sit down. She felt sick and shaken up. Sitting on the wall, she took some deep breaths, straightened her back and told herself she could do this. She had come a long way in the last two years since it had happened.

Picking up her luggage Moana made her way into the town, and knew she wanted some food. She wasn't going to wait for the meet-up, she needed to eat something to nourish her soul, and the moment she thought of something to nourish her soul, there right in front of her was a vegan gluten-free café with a board outside with the words 'nourish your soul' written on it. Well who was she to argue with that! She sat down and enjoyed a turmeric latte and quinoa salad with mango and walnuts. She was a happy woman.

Her time in this new location led her to different depths of her soul. She made friends, ended up living with the woman she had wanted to meet for a month whilst they worked side by side on their businesses. They were soul sisters of a different kind, sea sisters and driven to make a difference in the world; one healing the ocean and the other receiving the healing of the ocean. It was a beautiful combination and their laughter infectious.

The clicking and clacking of the keys on their keyboards tap tapped away as they created powerful movements across the planet. There were times when Moana would dive even deeper into her soul, crying from the abyss of darkness that the sign she had seen on her way out of the ferry terminal had pulled her into. There were days when she would hide away in her room, the days it would rain like the heavens were crying with her. There were days when she would walk along the beach, wind in her hair, taking steps forward so the darkness could be removed by the fierce Atlantic winds. Her sea brother, a friend of the woman she stayed with, saw her pain and shared profound wisdom with Moana that she was not expecting but so grateful to receive.

Sitting in the sun, writing, creating, and healing, looking out to the horizon she called in her next passage across the ocean. One that would make her reflect deeper on her beauty and make her question her commitment to leaving Joe all over again.

But how could she question it, she had felt so great and purged so much, but that's the thing with the healing process, you think you are there and BAM! Smacked back down on your arse and time to reflect and grow even more, almost as if God is playing with you just to test you and make sure you are really sure you are ready to let go, and go to the next level; whatever that means.

With her bags packed and heading to the marina, she had to smile, she was back where she had started when she left the UK. In the same grotty vomit and the irony was not lost on her as she had come full circle to move on to the next phase of her journey in the literal and the physical. The day of departure arrived, and the sky was black, the winds were up and there was a sensation she had not had before. Was it because this was going to be her first time in a storm this strong? Was it because the other members of the crew were loading alcohol on the boat? She wasn't sure, but she put it down to nerves at not having sailed in these conditions before.

Others in the marina were not leaving and many said they were crazy for leaving, but the captain gave the go ahead and off they sailed. A few hours into the ocean crossing they hit the storm with gusto, and it was time to bring down the sails, well past due the time but the captain had ignored her and chosen to bring the sails down later. She was sent up on deck with her fellow crew member and the next thing she knew she was hanging over the side of the boat, attached only by her lifeline and her legs banging against the side of the boat. Her feet were in the water and out of nowhere came the hand of her crew member and she heard herself say, "I've lost my teeth!" as she spat out the chalky remnants of what had been her beautiful teeth just moments before.

Looking in the mirror at her missing teeth, she cried. Her beautiful smile gone, her mouth all swollen and the fear of not being lovable returned with vengeance and made her miss the man she had walked away from just months earlier after so much soul searching. Would he be worried about her? What would he say if he saw her now, or would he repeat a similar statement he made to her in Italy of, "You're not so fucking beautiful now bitch, are you!" before mocking her more. She should have listened to her intuition. She should have walked away from this trip, but she didn't. Nothing she could do to change it, and nothing of her front teeth left; but the most important thing was she was alive… and her boys still had their mum.

The captain finally made the choice to turn around and head back to the safest marina, and Moana couldn't help chuckle to herself at the sense of humour the Universe seemed to have. They were heading into Cadiz; she would have to walk around the town looking for a dentist in the very place she had her first holiday with Joe and the first place he left her alone to be raped. Whether that was his intention or not didn't really matter. He had left her alone after she had hit her head after falling on the hard cobbled streets, and now she was facing the demons of her mind like she had done in the city of Sheffield when she had surprised her boys with her return back to the UK.

Once the boat had arrived and they were safely in the marina, it was time to sleep. They would go find a dentist in the morning so she could get an assessment done.

Walking around the town took her all the strength she could muster, and the memories were cascading thick and fast. Wonderful memories, beautiful memories, laughter, hugs and kisses, him asking her what kind of wedding dress she would wear, the romantic walks in the warm night air, and the garbage man who had raped her.

He was loud and clear in her head now, and his face no longer distorted. Memories of the flamenco bar, and her tripping over the cobbles hitting her head on the floor and blacking out. Nothing else until she saw his face, and then the morning after when Joe came in from clubbing. The sky was as overcast as her emotions and she refused to be beaten. She would not be beaten. She was going to heal from this and so she allowed the silent tears to roll down her face, pretending it was the cold air in her eyes.

Her fellow crew member, the one who saved her life, told her, "Just let it go, just cry if you want to. It is okay to cry." And he held her in his arms whilst she cried. He thought she was crying because of her teeth but she was crying because of all of it. Her teeth, her lack of confidence in her inner beauty that would outshine whether she had teeth or not, crying for the rape and crying because she was grieving for the relationship she had lost, but never really had in the first place. She was crying because she had brought that man into her life; she was crying because she had had the courage to face all of her fears and even take responsibility for her part in the relationship breaking down in an email she had sent to Joe just a week after leaving the UK.

She always took responsibility for her part in things, it was the grown up and respectful thing to do. Taking ownership was all part of the healing process and the growth we need as humans as we evolve into the very best version of ourselves. She had not heard back from him. Why would she? He had only ever played her anyway, and he was not the kind of person to take responsibility for his actions because he was still a boy trapped in a mans body, unable to navigate the storms of life. As her tears subsided her fellow crew mate suggested they go for coffee and then back to the boat, arriving back at the boat just in time before the heavens opened.

Lying in her bunk that night she went through everything that had happened in the last 48 hours. The uncertainty about leaving in the storm, and with the

people she was now on board with, she should have
listened to her intuition instead of being eager to get to her
next location. That said she was glad in some ways it had
all happened because she had been able to face a part of
her trauma and then release it, in the arms of a total
stranger. A man had held her whilst she released all the
emotions which had not been released since that night,
something Joe should have done, but didn't. Just being held
by a man and feeling safe in his arms was a truly wonderful
experience, one she had needed for this next level of
healing.

She journaled all the thoughts and emotions coming
up for her, and then she grabbed her phone and deleted
every photo she had of them both together, all the photos
of him alone, and all the photos of her looking into the
camera with thoughts of him on her mind. She did the
same on her laptop: delete, delete, delete. With each press
of that delete button she grew in power. If the photos were
not there, she couldn't access them. If the photos were not
there they could not be seen whilst searching for other
photos.

With each deletion, she set an intention, whilst
remembering how he had shamed her for exploring her
own body, telling her how disgusting it was. He had loved it
when they had first been together, was aroused by it, but
then after he chose celibacy he told her it was shameful
when a woman explored her own body. It wasn't shameful
for anyone to discover their own body, find out what
turned them on and what they liked and disliked. It made
love-making even more beautiful with another, and was a
healthy part of the spiritual journey, although some

religions and cultures thought the act of exploring ones body was shameful.

Bringing herself to orgasm, whether through touch or mental magic as she referred to it, was what made her discover parts of her beauty and her gratitude and awe of what a body was capable of. Joe taking away the physical intimacy may have been a way to develop another side of their relationship, but he had used it as a weapon against her. To shame her, to tell her she was addicted to sex, and the times he would call her into the bathroom and start talking with her whilst he lay in the bath holding his cock, and she wouldn't look at him, he would mock her. Ask her what the problem was, and then get annoyed with her because all he "wanted to do was fucking talk!"

Choosing celibacy when single is one thing, but to choose it without discussion when in a relationship with someone is completely different. It affects both parties and both need to agree with it, it's not like choosing to go vegan or give up smoking, but even then a couple in a healthy relationship would discuss it with each other.

This trip had taken her on an even deeper journey of self-discovery, of releasing more of the hold he had on her and had released pent up emotions and fear over what had happened.

What had happened in Cadiz was now left in Cadiz. Chapter closed.

SEVENTEEN

THE WOMB HEALING

Arrival at the island of the boat delivery, Moana was met with the sea parents of the sea sister she had lived with for a month. They both gave her hugs and held her, breathed strength into her and took her away from the captain who was in the process of blaming her for the accident because she had wanted to leave. Another man shirking his responsibility, and one that had nearly caused Moana death. No doubt had she gone overboard he would have denied any responsibility and laid all the blame on Moana.

She stayed with her new friends for a few nights on their boat and had a wonderful time, swapping stories and supporting each other in different ways, and then she was invited for lunch with another woman on her boat, who had heard of her story through the sailing network. They went out to lunch and this woman helped her find a great dentist, and off Moana went to get her teeth fixed.

The charter company she had delivered the boat for were not interested in compensating her, even though it was their responsibility, and even though she had delivered the boat free of charge. They had told her that they had not known she was on the boat and should not have been on it, so they took no responsibility. What was it with men not taking responsibility these days? Why did they keep showing up in her life? What did she need to heal within herself to stop attracting these men?

Several days of being on the island, staying on a boat AirBnB, it was coming up to Christmas, and with the next boat delivery across the Atlantic not due until the New Year, she chose to surprise the boys again. Flying back to see them, she was full of excitement, and this time she felt stronger than ever before – until she flew over the landmass of the UK. The negative energy hit her hard and felt suffocating. The landscape may be beautiful but there was just something she was not vibing with anymore. Her boys were surprised to see her, and the dogs so excited they both wet themselves, thankfully on the lino of the kitchen floor near the back door.

She managed to stay for the birthday of her youngest and then headed back to the boat ready for the trip. This trip back to the UK was insightful and left her reflecting a lot on what the future held for her. She had research to do and plans to make.

Arriving back at the boat, an ocean trial was completed with the husband of the wife who had invited her to join them, and sadly the husband and wife team chose to tell her the day before departure that they didn't want her to go with them. She had passed up several opportunities to make the crossing, and now they were dropping her? She asked them why. They said she talked about her achievements too much. She told them she was only answering their questions, what was she supposed to do, ignore them? Dumb herself down? Hide who she was? Play small just because the wife hadn't done anything since she had completed her degree years before and waited around on a boat for her husband to fly back to after being at work making more money than his dad?

No. She was done playing small. Done hiding who she was just because other people couldn't hack it. She was done with the lack of integrity and once again, she chose to go inwards and find out why she had attracted these people. She realised she had been shaken and disorientated when she first met this woman who offered her a passage, and the moment she had stepped back into her power, this woman had become intimidated by her. She noticed how many women were the same, and she noticed when she looked at her business plans this had come up as one of the things she had wanted to help empower women, and so it made perfect sense that she would be faced with this.

The only difference between Moana and a lot of women though was the choices she made each and every day to be brave, to be confident, to take herself on, to dive deep into her soul and release herself from all the excuses she made to hold herself back. She wanted to be successful. She wanted to provide an amazing life for her boys and she wanted to keep travelling, and she wanted to break free of the cycle of hiding who she was. Because how on earth could she help other women shine their light, and achieve their dreams if she didn't show them how she was living her dream life, shining her light?

She had purged a lot of the darkness. She had even passed the one-year marker of the date of the gang rape without even noticing. She had been so pre-occupied with everything she was doing, and who she was becoming it had come and gone without her paying attention to it. This made her happy, and this was something for her to celebrate. So she booked herself on another ocean journey, by herself as passenger, going to another island which would have some life changing moments which would mean she would be transformed beyond measure, and really step out of the shadows of who she was being, so she could become the woman she was born to become.

On this island she was about to give birth so many times, in a variety of ways that she would also remember this island as the Island of Magic.

She had to wait for many months before she could cross her next ocean, so it was time to look for a place to stay for the duration. AirBnB become her most trusted companion and introduced her to some amazing places.

After a few weeks she met a new family and was invited to stay with them until her new apartment appeared. Geri was a huge amount of fun, singing and dancing, and they would stay up late into the night sewing and making costumes, and Geri even introduced Moana to a TV programme; not to mention the art of falling asleep five minutes into the programme starting.

Moana would become Aunty to Kevin and Marnie, and many family meals enjoyed. She missed her children, missed cooking for them, but she knew this trip had developed them into competent solo travellers. Both boys were growing into confident trustworthy young men and young men Moana was incredibly proud of. The more she achieved, the more they cheered her on, the more they told her she was not to go back, the world needed her as much as they did; and they were the lucky ones as they got her as their mum… and all the fab holidays around the world.

When she wasn't with her boys and had finally moved into her own place she focused so much on her business and her healing journey. Living with Geri, Kevin and Marnie had been great, but she needed time alone to dive deeper into the purging of the toxic energies in her womb and the deeper emotional pain she was feeling. She was also using her business as a way to protect herself. If she was working all day and night then she had a good excuse to not socialise.

In her mind it wasn't safe to socialise, it wasn't safe to drink, and it certainly wasn't safe to be out at night. Hiding away in her apartment, hiding in her business, not letting people in other than a few select friends, each who knew a little bit of what she was going through was enough. Any more than that, and it was too much. Yeah she talked about lots of stuff, but it was all a smoke screen for what was really going on, much like the distraction technique parents have been using with their kids for years.

Moana wanted to cleanse her womb space, the space of creation and receiving, in so many ways. Looking up womb healing, cord cuttings and timeline healings she came across a woman called Sandra Rolus, a woman who was well known in this field of work and had quite a huge following. One night, Moana put on the three-hour womb healing meditation she found on YouTube, and for the next few hours she felt like she was in labour. She felt the pains in her cervix, the pain of needing to push something out, and having given birth before, she knew what giving birth was like. The noises of labour, the pushing, the sweating, the screaming, whatever was inside of her was coming out and it was coming out of her with force.

After the meditation she needed to go to the toilet and it hurt, just like it had after giving birth to her eldest. It was uncomfortable to walk, and yet she felt so powerful, just like she had the night she gave birth to her firstborn. The next day she slept, tired, exhausted, and serene, almost as if she were in another world. She snuggled up in her bed and just allowed herself the time she needed and just did whatever she felt called to do.

The following day she felt emotional and needed to go to the beach. For some reason she took her crystals with her. She didn't know much about crystals, but she knew the properties of some of them, in a very beginner kind of way. She had heard it was a good idea to wash them in the ocean before placing them on certain parts of your body, not that she needed any excuse to go into the ocean, but taking her crystals in with her gave her a different sensation, or was it all psychosomatic? Moana also didn't know the 'rules' of crystals or where to place them on her body, so she just went with what felt right. Lying there with the sun on her skin, the sand beneath her, the sound of the waves crashing on the beach, she smiled, deeply. She noticed her eyes were leaking. She didn't think she was crying, but with the tears falling from her eyes, she was crying, or rather her soul was releasing whatever it needed to release.

She stayed there on the beach, reading, journaling and playing in the ocean. She had got used to swimming and floating in the ocean by herself. She loved it. A few others didn't like it so much when she was deep in a water meditation and had been floating for a while, and they had to come over to check she was okay. But this was her time, for her to enjoy, and she was in love with her own company. She was in love with the results her clients were having, in love with the progress she was having and excited about the future.

As she dried off in the summer sun, she began to really look out to sea, and all of a sudden she realised how she could truly turn the negatives that had happened to her, into a positive for her, and as a way of helping to heal others who had been through a similar experience, and experiences far worse than hers. She was going to use her talents to speak about the pain, the trauma, the healing processes, the way in which the global dialogue needs to change and how what happened to her, could happen to anyone, not just women and girls who wear next to nothing and sleep around. It was understanding those kinds of behaviours, diving deep into the systematic cover ups, the corruption within the social care and policing system. She was going to expose it all and create a powerful shift in the global discourse.

The name of *The Sacral Series* dropped into her mind, she saw the nine books and she knew what she needed to do.

She dived deeper into the healing videos and meditations Sandra Rolus shared. She did cord cuttings with the Archangel Michael and the Archangel Gabriel. She listened to deep Shamanic drumming and established new gridlines within her energetic field with women such as Gaby Kowalski.

Moana had always known that the phrase 'the sky's the limit' was a massive limitation in itself. You only had to look at the cosmos and know there were galaxies, worm holes, black holes and nebulas far beyond our reach. Moana knew there were no limits and had always known she was not of this world; how could she be when she had never felt like she belonged anywhere on earth? Nowhere felt right, but she hadn't been everywhere yet, so how did she know where home was if she had not explored the world? Limiting ourselves to just one place and calling it home made no sense to Moana, it just didn't. It felt comfortable, and yeah it was nice being recognised and having people know your name and wave at you in the street, but that could happen anywhere and everywhere.

She liked this new sense of freedom and made contact with the tax office about leaving the UK for good and asked how to go about it, putting things in place for her to haul anchor and be a really true free spirit.

Thinking about how else to heal her body, she remembered one of the reasons she had the copper coil inside of her was because it prevented her from getting pregnant. Well if she wasn't in a relationship and had learnt to protect herself, then there was no reason for her to keep the coil in. She meditated on it and asked the Universe to send her a sign if this was the right thing to do. It would certainly help get rid of the copper contamination in her body, even though medical professionals said it was safe, it was still something that didn't belong in her body. What was the point of eating organic, non-processed food, not smoking or drinking alcohol and exercising if she still had the coil her body? Expecting to come across a doctor or an article whilst she was researching other things, Moana just left things up to the Universe to work its magic.

The next morning whilst working in the café, she noticed there were some gluten-free biscuits. She never bought biscuits, but for some reason on this morning she did. Back in her apartment after making a delicious salad for lunch, she felt this excruciating pain in her uterus. It brought tears to her eyes and made her double over in pain.

"What the fuck…?" exclaimed Moana, feeling dizzy and as if she were about to pass out. Making her way doubled over to the toilet she sat down. Head in her hands and her undies around her ankles just in case something happened – what, she didn't know, but something – anything might happen after that pain, she found herself needing to pee. And it burned, it stung but then it went cool, almost refreshing and like she was entering the ocean. As she wiped herself, she felt something scratch and touching herself she discovered the coil had made its way out of her cervix all the way to the lips of her vagina. She didn't need to pull it; she just took it out and looked at it in disbelief. How on earth had that happened? She looked and smiled, she knew she had a powerful mind, she knew that when mind, body and soul aligned amazing things happened, but WOW. JUST WOW!

As she washed her hands and placed a panty liner in her knickers, she put the kettle on for a cup of tea and reached for the biscuits. She felt like she needed the sugar to sort her head out, because in less than ten minutes she was being interviewed. She needed some colour in her cheeks and needed a pick me up, and as sugar always made her feel a bit high, this would prove to be the reason she had randomly purchased biscuits that morning.

With the podcast completed, she took herself to bed, she was wiped out. Not only had she given birth to something and expelled what was inside of her, she had just birthed the coil out of her body in less than 24 hours of asking the Universe for confirmation or a sign that it should be removed. She slept soundly that night, and most of the next day. A week later she noticed that her body felt different, her face had broken out in spots and she was a lot more focused, had a lot more clarity.

Had the coil been poisoning her that much? She had also noticed that since the night she gave birth to the entity within her, she had not had the sensation of a baby still moving around inside of her, something she had experienced since her first son was born. She had always felt it, especially underneath her heart. She had wondered if the baby was a twin of some kind, but had never mentioned it to anyone other than her doctor, who had told her that it was common for mothers to miss the sensation of a baby inside of them that they sometimes imagined or experienced the sensation of a baby moving inside of them; not dissimilar to a person who had lost a limb, they would sometimes feel that the limb was still there.

She was now even more fascinated to see how this whole manifestation process could go. She had manifested so much with her journaling and meditation over the last year, and now the trade winds were picking up, she needed to manifest a trip to the other side of the Atlantic, thinking she may end up in the tropics, but knowing she wanted to learn more about the Mayan Oracles, she just let the universe decide where she was most needed, or what would be the best location for her.

Within an hour of finishing journaling, she opened up her laptop and then her emails, and there staring her in the face was a trip of a lifetime that would take her so much closer to so many goals. She simply booked it and said yes, yes to the adventure, yes to herself, yes to trusting the process, and yes to being free of all that was holding her back.

Moana was free, and she had made the journey home back to self, the place she truly belonged all along.

FINAL WORDS

So many of us struggle on by ourselves, pushing down our pain, ignoring who we are and pushing our goals and dreams to one side.

We very rarely reach out for help, thinking what we are going through is too much for others to handle, that it is something people do not want to know, wouldn't be comfortable in knowing and feeling like we would be a burden.

Some subjects we push under the carpet, thinking if we ignore it, it will go away. We start to isolate ourselves and sink into depression, often living a life in which the traumas we have experienced control our futures, giving a twisted kind of victory to those who inflicted or caused the traumas in our lives.

Some of the content in this book is not an easy read, and for those who have recognised it as my story, it will have been a very difficult read. I have chosen to share my story, so I can lead the way for others to share theirs. So we can change the way we heal from generations of abuse, rape and trauma, in the hope that we can break this negative pattern and cycle so that future generations can live life without abuse, rape and trauma.

The Sacral Series is nine real life stories, with identities changed so I can protect those who gave their stories for me to write. I have revealed my identity because it did not feel authentic for me as the author to write and speak about the subjects in the nine books without giving context of my own experience.

If there is one thing I have learnt along this journey to healing is that the healing is never done. It is messy, it is painful and when you think you are done, there is always another layer lurking. This is not to say don't bother starting the healing process, because when you do, you discover a life of joy, abundance and a community of people who will support you and lift you up to your highest high.

Life is not meant to be lived alone. It is not meant to be lived in fear or pain. Life is for living, loving, and laughing and as I always say, and fully embody with every cell of my body, live to laugh, and laugh to live, because when we laugh every day we gift ourselves the best healing there is.

Joy.

Sadness cannot exist where there is joy.

Fear cannot exist where there is joy.

Hatred cannot exist where there is joy.

Loneliness cannot exist where there is joy.

So, embrace joy through gratitude, and remember when we reach out for love and support from others, when we love ourselves so much we overflow with love, we are able to love others from this overflow and teach others how to love us, and love themselves.

And it is from this space that we get to serve humanity from our highest levels of existence.

Sending you all so much love, courage, strength, and hope, now and always,

Thank you for choosing to read this book, it means the world to me, and I hope you have taken away some ideas and insights which will help you or someone you know live a much more fulfilled life.

With gratitude, for you and to you,

Dawn

GRATITUDE

No book is complete without gifting gratitude and acknowledgements to others who have helped us along our journey, especially when it comes to revealing truths about ourselves, or exploring challenging and difficult subjects.

Sexual abuse, rape, gang rape and narcissism are some of the most toxic elements of today's society, and they are not new. In fact, they have been in existence for generations, centuries and if we do not speak up and share our truths, the journey's we have taken to recovery and healing, then these patterns will continue for centuries to come; and the pain, trauma and suffering we have been through will have amounted for nothing.

I am so blessed to have some wonderful friends who have supported me on this journey as I have discovered parts of myself, learnt about various aspects of the human condition and dived deep into my own soul to break patterns of behaviour, heal ancestral wounds and belief systems.

This has not been an easy journey due to the nature of

the subjects contained within these pages, and the pages of the subsequent books that follow Moana and her journey. Sexual abuse, rape and the law are very heavy subjects, and there needs to be an element of delicacy when telling these kinds of stories.

Names and locations have been changed for a variety of reasons, and as with any work of fiction based on factual events, there may be identifying factors. For anyone to heal on a deep level, they must speak their truth, and for humanity to heal as a whole, stories like the ones you will read in *The Sacral Series* need to be shared.

I personally would not have been able to write these books without the support of my ex-husband, Omar. He has stood by me, even though we are no longer married, supported me on my own personal journey, taken care of our children, and been there to support our children as these stories become public. The long phone calls, the words of encouragement, the perspective, and the care he has given me – gave me the courage, on many occasions, to keep going. He is an incredible guy, and a very dear friend, a great father, and the best ex-husband I could ever have wished for.

I would also like to thank my friend Charlie Burrows. She won't expect to read her name in this book, but to not mention her wouldn't be right; she did, after all, come up with the subtitle for the book! She has held space for me whilst I have explored the ideas and concepts, as well as shared my own personal experiences. Her encouraging messages and virtual hugs on an almost daily basis, the endless cups of tea across multiple time zones have been invaluable. We have shared laughter, shamanic healings, cord cutting and deep healing meditations with each other, and I am so very grateful for her constant support and friendship on my journey.

To my dear friend Renelle McPherson who, other than Linda, was the first to know I was to write this book in its current form. The first friend I revealed the entire contents of the story to, and who asked me some really difficult questions which I avoided like the plague, until resistance was futile. The work Renelle does in this world, healing deep trauma, has helped me beyond measure. She is a woman who brings a smile, tears and a whole lot of love and laughter to my life. She has been there with me every step of the way over the last five years, and seen my life transform as I have dived deeper and deeper into my soul. Holding space for each other, calling each other forward; and cleansing our spaces together both internally and externally has been one hell of a journey, and we are both only really just beginning.

For agreeing to write the foreword for me, and the men and women around the world who will be introduced to her work, I offer my deepest gratitude to Sandra Rolus, a Timeline Trauma Release Facilitator, Karmic and Ancestral Healer. Her meditations had a profound effect on my own healing journey, my understanding of the traumas we carry within our DNA, our womb spaces and through the generations. It was following one of her three-hour meditations that *The Sacral Series* was conceived. To have her write the foreword and have her share her wisdom with you at the start of this series is an absolute honour and a privilege, and I know my work with her is far from over.

For his brotherly love, quantum healing and new moon breathwork as I came to the final chapters of this book, I have to thank Korey Carpenter. Reaching out to him as the remnants of trauma, negative emotions and tears fell away was just what was needed as this book came to its end during the new full moon of September 1st, 2020.

My gratitude also goes to Jerry Lampson for another first-class design on the cover work. He is a true genius when it comes to interpreting my ideas and delivering show stopping book covers. How he unravels my thoughts I have no idea, but I am glad he does, and I am glad to have this man in my life.

Then there's Linda Diggle, my right-hand woman. The woman who focuses my mind, supports my crazy publishing deadlines, and makes everything flow with each. Linda has become so very dear to me, and held space for me as I have unpacked, processed, and fathomed out not just the visions for my books, but my business, my hopes and dreams, and my sanity. No easy task by anyone's standards. She is my fellow bookworm, my 'one spacer' to my 'two spacer' and I love her immensely.

To have the full support of my mum and dad, the reality check and grounding from their no-nonsense, feet on the ground reminders, and hilarious conversations with my mum, means the world to me. It can't be easy for them to read my life in print and have the locals make comments and have themselves put in the local spotlight, but still they support me, encourage me and tell me they are proud (well not so much my dad, he is a man of few words, but still, I know he is proud of me from the looks he gives and the 'ummming' and 'arrghing' he does).

My deepest gratitude of course goes to the two gorgeous souls I have the honour and the privilege to be a mother to. The two amazing young men, Khaalid and Naasir, who light up my life, make me giggle, cry and show up each and every day to help make the world a better place. No longer boys, these two incredible souls inspire me to become a better woman than I was yesterday, a better leader for women everywhere and the voice so many women need to hear and want to hear. To them, and for them, I am the most grateful. They make me feel like the luckiest woman alive, because without them and their words of encouragement, the coaching they turn back around on me, the dares and challenges they cheekily give me, I would not have achieved half of what I have achieved. Awlaadi, ana behebik awi awi awi jidan awi, Mama xx

And finally thank you to all of you who have chosen to purchase this book, for taking a leap of faith in me, in yourself and being part of the journey of healing humanity together. The story you are about to read is not just my story, or your story, but the story of many women, the world over.

With so much love and gratitude to you all,
Dawn x

ABOUT SANDRA ROLUS

My name is Sandra Rolus and I am a time-line trauma release facilitator and teacher trainer. I help people all over the world to release their birth, childhood, and sexual trauma on a deep energetic level, during online workshops, multiple-day in-person retreats and private sessions.

As a teacher I am also an eternal student. For decades I have been on a personal healing journey and next to that I trained with experts in various fields with the intent to reach deeper levels of awareness so I can continue to grow as a facilitator.

It's my absolute pleasure to make my work available to everybody and that is why I created a YouTube channel with a large variety of free guided sessions. The techniques I use are my three-core signature healing modalities:

- Sexual de-Armouring
- Soul re-Birthing
- Trans-Generational & Ancestral Healing

I use my signature sessions in combination with shamanic journeying, breath work and timeline re-imprinting techniques.

instagram.com/sandra.rolus

youtube.com/SandraRolus

ABOUT DAWN BATES

With 20+ years of entrepreneurial experience, coaching and leading individuals and teams to outstanding results, Dawn Bates is one of the world's best kept secrets, and for good reason. Delivering impeccable service to her clients means she is selective in who she works with; her strong moral compass guides her to the projects she chooses to take on.

Dawn's repertoire of work is vast and her inquisitive mind astounding, bringing fresh insights and perspectives from 20 years of international travel and working in the UK, Europe, the Middle East and Australasia, with clients spanning five continents, multiple ethnicities, cultures and languages.

With a passion for leadership and cultural diversity, Dawn brings a wealth of knowledge and experience like no other. Her expertise lies in making you rethink your life and the world we live in, harnessing the deepest freedom of all: your own truth.

As well as being an international bestselling author, author strategist and ghostwriter, Dawn specialises in developing brand expansion, step change strategies and global visions, underpinned by her profound wisdom, truth slaying approach, high energy and trademark giggle.

She writes for various magazines, and when not sailing

around the world on yachts, she appears on various media channels highlighting and discussing important subjects in today's society.

She's an authority on leading others to create exceptional results by igniting the passions and fire deep within, shifting individuals and teams from disconnection, fear, feelings of imposter and self-doubt, to confidence, connection and courage to speak, live and work powerfully together with others.

To find out more, please visit www.dawnbates.com where you can listen to the podcasts which accompany this book and the entire Sacral Series collection of conversations and books.

If you have purchased a copy of this book, I would love for you to send me a selfie of you and my book.

Tag me on:

facebook.com/RealDawnBates

instagram.com/realdawnbates

twitter.com/realdawnbates

linkedin.com/in/dawnbates

…so I can thank you in person.

Ciao for now mi amore, and be blessed always x

www.ingramcontent.com/pod-product-compliance
Lightning Source LLC
Chambersburg PA
CBHW020253030426
42336CB00010B/741